SO-ARO-649

ESEA TITLE I PHASE 2
1976 - 1977

black gold

BY THE SAME AUTHOR

Susan and Her Classic Convertible

Wheels and Pistons: The Story of the Automobile

The Narc

Dave White and the Electric Wonder Car

black gold
the story of oil

by w.e. butterworth

four winds press new york

LIBRARY OF CONGRESS CATALOGING IN PUBLICATION DATA

Butterworth, William E.
  Black gold.

  SUMMARY: Traces the history of oil from its use by the
ancient Sumerians through the present energy crisis, with
emphasis on the men who fought for control of the oil industry.
  1. Petroleum—History—Juvenile literature. [1. Petroleum—
History. 2. Petroleum industry and trade—History] I. Title.
TN870.B97   338.2′7′28209   74–28479
ISBN 0–590–07297–8

PUBLISHED BY FOUR WINDS PRESS
A DIVISION OF SCHOLASTIC MAGAZINES, INC., NEW YORK, N.Y.
COPYRIGHT © 1975 BY W. E. BUTTERWORTH
ALL RIGHTS RESERVED
PRINTED IN THE UNITED STATES OF AMERICA
LIBRARY OF CONGRESS CATALOG CARD NUMBER: 74–28479

1 2 3 4 5 79 78 77 76 75

black gold

chapter 1

THERE HAVE BEEN THREE ERAS IN THE HISTORY of oil. The first goes back before recorded history. The second goes back no more than three or four hundred years, and the third, the present, can be precisely dated as starting south of Beaumont, Texas, at 10:30 in the morning of January 10, 1901, when the gusher named "Spindletop" came in, providing people with more energy than they had dreamed possible.

In the third verse of the eleventh chapter of Genesis there is a reference to what we call petrocarbons, or bitumens, and what the ancients called "slime": ". . . And they had brick for stone, and slime they had for mortar." That was for building the Tower of Babel. Three chapters later (Genesis 14:10) there is the first recorded oil field location: "And the vale of Siddim was full of slime-pits; and the Kings of Sodom and Gomorrah fled, and fell there. . . ." The Bible tells us, too, that when Noah built his ark, he applied two coats of bitumen outside and one coat inside.

On the walls of Egyptian tombs dating back to 4000 B.C. there are drawings showing that the Egyptians used oil to prepare meals and a thousand years later, some three thousand years before Jesus of Nazareth, the Sumerians used asphalt as a glue under inlaid mosaic walls and floors. In Ur of Chaldea during that time, bitumen was selling for about thirty dollars a ton.

What was it the ancients used, where did they get it, and more important, where did it come from? Most scientists agree that petroleum is organic. Hundreds of millions of years ago, the theory goes, when most of the earth was covered with water, the oceans teemed with tiny aquatic plants and animals.

Countless billions of them died over a period of hundreds of millions of years and sank to the bottom of the seas. There they mixed with clay and mud, forming what scientists call marine sediment. From time to time disturbances dumped large quantities of sand and mud on top of the marine sediment, forming it into layers—a layer of sediment, then a layer of clay or sand or a mixture of both, then another layer of sediment. The layers built up, and the ones on the bottom were compressed by the weight of the layers above them.

Millions of years passed, and the buckling of the earth's crust (and probably its interior, too) continued. The water receded from some areas, and the bottom of the ocean in other areas grew deeper. Vast quantities of water were frozen and captured at the poles, and a chemical reaction took place. The vast pressures present and the pressures created by the buckling of the earth generated heat, which converted the chemical substances in the dead and decaying vegetable and animal matter (hydrogen and carbon, primarily) into what we call oil.

Scientists generally believe that petroleum is a fossil fuel. At the same time, it's called a mineral fuel, because much of our supply of petroleum is contained in the pores of one form of rock or another.

Chemically, "crude" petroleum (as opposed to "refined") is made up of hydrogen and carbon combined in molecules of different sizes and arrangements. All forms of petroleum are hydrocarbons of a different volatility, based on the number of hydrogen atoms in relation to the number of carbon atoms.

Small molecules (1 to 4 carbon atoms to 1 of hydrogen) make up the gases. Four to 10 make up gasoline; when the ratio is 1 to 50, we have lubricating oils and light fuel oils. When the ratio gets up to 100:1 or 500:1, we have heavy fuels, waxes, and asphalts.

The great bulk of oil is found far beneath the surface. Of course, this is relative; 20,000 feet straight down is not much considering the diameter of the earth, but it's a long way when people are trying to drill that far. Some petroleum, because of the way the earth buckled, is right at the surface and, in a few cases, comes bubbling through it.

This is what the ancients found. Petroleum came to the surface and seeped out into natural basins, flowing like water. The lighter components of it were refined away by nature. Gasoline (which occurs naturally in petroleum) will evaporate rapidly at about eighty-five degrees Fahrenheit.

When the gasoline had evaporated, a substance thicker than the original surface petroleum remained. And then the "lighter" portions (fractions) of that began to evaporate, too, until finally there was left a thick, black, sticky, often foul-smelling material. Some brave soul experimented with it and was soon able to announce that "oil and water don't mix." Because they don't mix, oil could be used to keep water in something (applied to the outside of a wooden container) or out of something (applied to the hull of a boat, as Noah applied it to his ark). Since it was also sticky, it could be used to bind a variety of things together, from the Sumerians' intricate mosaic inlays to a road, where it would hold rocks in place and be impermeable to rain.

The "pure" bitumen worth thirty dollars a ton in Ur of Chaldea probably was petroleum which had naturally fractioned until it was just the way the Chaldeans wanted it for whatever purpose they had in mind. At that price, most likely it was used as a tile cement or a waterproofing substance.

Around 1500 B.C. the latest word in lighting consisted of the censer or firepan. A natural petroleum liquid, which had the desired volatility (it would burn slowly and not flame dangerously or explode), was burned to give off light. (Some historians feel that the censers and firepans burned rendered animal fat.) This lamp had a long life, with improvements here and there, until it was replaced by the wick-lamp, which worked by drawing the flammable liquid up a wick by capillary action. This lamp is still with us, most obviously in the kerosene lantern.

Five hundred years after the first interior lighting using a petroleum fuel came into being, around 900 B.C., the Chinese were the first to put natural gas to use. Natural gas is nothing more than a light fraction of petroleum which comes from the ground in a gaseous form, ready for use as is. The Chinese used it for heat, not light, and they brought what had to be heated to the source of the natural gas, rather than piping the gas elsewhere.

The obvious advantages of gas as a fuel were apparent to the Chinese. It was a significant improvement over anything else they had, and it didn't have to be chopped like wood. The next step was obvious; moving the gas from where it appeared naturally to where it could be used more conveniently. Soon the Chinese were building simple but functional pipelines.

The demand for gas grew in proportion to human awareness that it was a first-class fuel. By 600 B.C., Confucius was able to write of wells several hundred feet deep along the Tibetan border of China. If the drillers didn't find gas in the wells, they generally found water. If they were looking for water and found gas, that was all right, too.

In 206 B.C., a spring of oil was found, near Yenchang, in Shensi Province, China and its products were put to use as grease and for lamps. A hundred years later the Romans marveled at a "flaming fountain" they came across while chasing the savage Gauls near what is now Grenoble, France.

In the first century of the Christian era both Pliny and Plutarch make reference to oil in their writings. Plutarch wrote of
oil in what is today known as the Kirkuk Field, and Pliny reported that "Sicilian oil" was used to light the Temple of Jupiter.
Pliny's report is the first positive identification of petroleum used
as a lubricant. By 600 A.D. the Japanese, with picks and shovels,
had dug wells in search of oil to depths approaching 900 feet,
and there are indications that they also found gas and put it to
use.

During the same century the Romans used petroleum for the
first time in warfare. They destroyed the Saracen fleet in 670
with oil, throwing flaming containers of it at the Saracen's
wooden ships, which burned. Eighty years later, in 750, the
Arab and Mongol armies were using both flaming grenades
(small vessels containing burning oil) and the ancestor of the
flamethrower in military operations.

And around 800 A.D., the first oil "miracle worker"—the first
of a long line of charlatans, fakes, and mountebanks—appeared
in Japan. Kobo Daish, a Japanese farmer who became an itiner-
ant mystic, apparently came across a flowing gas well near
Echigo and recognized it for what it was. He gathered a large
crowd of his believers (and some skeptics) at the site and announced that because he had divine powers there would be,
from that moment forward, an eternal flame sprouting from the
center of the earth, which he had ordered. He waved a flaming
torch in a suitably impressive manner, said the right magic
words, and lit the jet of escaping natural gas.

His act wouldn't have worked in China, however, because the
Chinese knew much more about natural gas. By 900 A.D. they
had working pipelines of bamboo catching gas at the well sites
and piping it where they wanted it to go. It was used for illumination, and no one thought it was magical.

In 967 A.D. across the world in Baku, in what is now the
Soviet Union but was then part of Persia (Iran), there was a

spontaneous combustion of gases from a naptha deposit.* It was spectacular, with flames shooting several hundred feet into the air and visible for miles. Most religious scholars believe that the spectacle had occurred before and that it had turned Zoroaster (628–551 B.C.) into a worshiper of fire. Vestiges of Zoroastrianism endure today.

The Chinese, meanwhile, were far more practical about petroleum and devoted their efforts to finding more of it. By 1100, using primitive means—often nothing but picks and shovels—they had reached depths over three thousand feet in searching for oil and gas. This was centuries before the West was to dig its first well.

Around the year 1250 Marco Polo wrote of seeing people going to the oil seepage areas at Baku (where flaming gases had so inspired Zoroaster) to collect oil. He said there were "streams of them." A century later, court records tell us, "eight pounds of petroleum" were delivered to King Edward III of England in his "chambers at Calais." The records do not tell us what he did with it, but the supposition is that he used it as vaseline.

By 1500 the ambitious Chinese had concluded that it made little sense to dig a hole with a shovel, when the oil they were seeking could come up through a hole only as big around as a man's arm. They began to experiment with drilling wells, rather than digging them, and soon, using primitive but quite ingenious equipment, they had reached two thousand feet. At the same

---

* The word "petroleum" first appears in medieval Latin, the source of the English word, about 1000 A.D., derived from the words for "rock oil." The most common ancient words for natural petroleum and its products were maltha, asphaltos (or asphaltum), bitumen, and naptha. Bitumen, asphalt, and naptha are still used today to describe a particular petroleum fraction. (For example, asphalt is one of the heaver petroleum fractions; naptha, a lighter fraction, is the proper term for cigarette-lighter fluid.)

time, the world's greatest inventor (who predicted the submarine and the helicopter as well as many other things) Leon-
ardo da Vinci, made a drawing of a machine to drill wells. It had
a four-legged derrick and a drill stem and looked very much like
the well derricks of the nineteenth and twentieth centuries.

In 1510 Columbus sent samples of asphalt from Trinidad to
Spain. Then in 1543 the De Soto expedition, en route south
toward Mexico along the coast of the Gulf of Mexico paused on
what is now the Texas coast between High Island and Sabine
Pass. They found a natural bed of asphalt and used it to coat the
leaking bottoms of their boats.

People were growing more and more aware of the oozing,
sometimes foul-smelling, sometimes gaseous material the earth
was bringing to its surface, but they had no idea what it was or
what to do with it. It wasn't until 1609, for example, that the
word "gas" itself appeared in the Western vocabulary. It was
coined by van Helmont, a Belgian chemist.

The East was somewhat ahead of us. It's obvious that if the
Chinese were using gas regularly for illumination and heating
purposes, they had a name for it. And four years after van Helmont coined the word "gas," a Japanese, Magara, was attempting to refine crude oil into an oil that would be suitable for
illuminating purposes.

Fourteen years after that, in 1627, we have the first reference
to oil in the United States as an interesting oddity, with no reference to any possible use for it. A Franciscan priest-explorer,
Joseph de la Roche d'Allion, traveling through upper New York
state near what is now Cuba, New York, wrote in his diary that
he had come across a "fontaine de bitume" (a fountain of oil).
About this time, however, the West began to catch up with the
East and then to surpass it both in practical applications of oil
and in petrocarbon chemistry.

In 1650 in Bacau, Moldavia (now Rumania) oil shafts dug
by hand began to produce, and in 1659 natural gas was dis-

covered by Thomas Shirley in Lancashire, England. Its availability was to have a major effect on the Industrial Revolution, as were other British scientific activities with fuel. An Anglican minister, the Rev. John Clayton, about 1670 began experimenting with the distillation of coal. He suspected that there was a more efficient means of releasing the energy in coal than by burning it. Another Englishman, Robert Boyle, was working with the same general thoughts in mind and in 1690 made a startling announcement: when coal is heated, it gives off a combustible gas. Every high school freshman knows this, but at that time it was a discovery of major importance and opened a new field of scientific inquiry.

As the eighteenth century opened, Peter the Great of Russia began an expansion program. In 1723 he conquered the Khanate of Baku in Persia (Iran). As soon as the military activity was over, he sent in a "master of refining" to take over the oil deposits for the Crown. But before the year was over, Peter the Great took government out and granted concessions to private entrepreneurs to seek, refine, and ship oil, giving a percentage to the Crown. The Baku fields remained in private hands until the Great Revolution of 1917–18, when the Soviet government took them over again, whereupon oil production promptly plummeted.

About fifty years later, a Swede, Peter Kalm, published a report of his travels in the wilderness of the British colonies. Included in his report was a map of what was then Pennsylvania. On the map he located the "oil springs" near Oil Creek. Those springs were to change humanity's entire way of life. Their location appeared again on a map published in London in 1755, not as precisely, but prophetically. Across the whole region of that part of Pennsylvania the cartographer wrote "petroleum."

In Philadelphia about this time and a little later, Benjamin Franklin was turning his amazing mind to the practical applications of oil. His concern at the time was with sailing vessels, which had a difficult time in rough water. He wondered what would happen if whale oil (whale blubber rendered into oil) were spread on the surface of stormy waters. He apparently didn't consider petroleum oils, and the idea wasn't a very good one, but it does show that Franklin had more than an inkling of the physical properties of oil.

In 1768 a Frenchman, Antoine Baume, developed systems to measure the specific gravity of liquids, one for liquids heavier than water, the other for liquids lighter than water. The next year in Paris Nicholas Joseph Cugnot rolled around the streets —not very far, not very fast—in a three-wheeled, steam-propelled carriage. He was an army officer, and the machine was designed to haul artillery, but it could, of course, haul people as well. It would never, people said, replace the horse. It might well be the first self-propelled vehicle, but it very probably was the last. Who needed it?

chapter 2

AS THE NINETEENTH CENTURY OPENED IN AMERICA, the talk of the scientific world was a Frenchman, Phillipe le Bon, who had been granted a patent for his technique of making gas. He heated coal in a closed vessel and withdrew the gases formed through a tube.

This offered immediate possibilities (lighting of streets and houses the most obvious), and little attention was paid to le Bon's second announcement that year, that he thought it was possible to generate power by compressing an air-gas mixture behind a piston and then exploding it to drive the piston.

He carried out experiments in which he succeeded both in compressing a gas-air mixture and in exploding it with an electric spark. In other words, he had invented the internal combustion engine, although no one then gave it a name.

What people were interested in was having lighted streets. In England in the early months of 1802, the public was given its first demonstration of gas lighting at the Soho Gas Works in London. Citizens of Baltimore, Maryland, got their first look at the new marvel on March 10, 1802, when it was demonstrated by Benjamin Henfry.

This was two years before the first steam locomotive took to the rails, and the first crack at that (in 1804 on the Merthyr Tidfil Railway) was a financial disaster. Clearly, people said, if God intended people to roll rapidly along steel rails, He would have provided them with wheels, not legs.

There was some feeling, too, that coal was intended to be burned in lumps, the way it had always been burned and that there was something questionable, if not downright dangerous, about extracting an invisible flammable gas from something like coal.

When Frederick Albert Winsor was granted the first British patent for the manufacture of gas in 1804, the first thing he had to do was give speeches and demonstrations to calm the public's fears. It wasn't until the next year that some avant-garde thinker suggested that food could be cooked with this gas.

In 1806, however, a reckless American, David Melville, of Newport, Rhode Island, apparently one of the earliest do-it-yourselfers, manufactured coal gas in his basement and used the gas to light his home. In the same year, the first gas main (between Haymarket and St. James's in London) was laid. It was made of sheets of lead formed around a log and then sealed.

In January 1807 Winsor felt that his public-relations efforts had been so successful that he could stage a large public demonstration of his coal gas. He lit up Pall Mall in London, and, to the astonishment of the population, there was neither an explosion nor a bolt of lightning to signify heavenly disapproval.

This was the first successful lighting of a public area, six months before Robert Fulton sailed his steamboat *Clermont* up the Hudson River against the tide, the beginning of the end for the sailboat.

At Oil Creek, Pennsylvania, meanwhile, oil was bringing two dollars a gallon. The method of recovery was simplicity itself. The water was dammed up; the oil floated to the surface; a blanket was thrown on the oil and the oil soaked up into it; the blanket was then retrieved and wrung out. A good worker could produce ten gallons a day this way, and at two dollars a gallon, that was a quick way to make a dollar.

The British had already begun to have a gas industry, but the only American working with gas was still David Melville. In 1812 Parliament chartered the London & Westminister Gas Light & Coke Company, the first gas company in the world. The same year Melville expanded his gas-lighting system to include a light on the street in front of his house. In March 1813 Melville was granted a patent for his gas-making technique and machinery, and then he installed gas lights in factories in Watertown and Providence, Massachusetts. The British countered by installing gas lights the full length of Westminister Bridge.

Baltimore, which had seen the first demonstration of gas lighting fourteen years before, became in 1816 the first American city to have gas lights on its streets. In Philadelphia the first commercial use of interior gas lighting was in the New Theatre.

But there were also obvious unpleasant results of people fooling around with nature. In 1818 oil escaped from a salt well in Wayne County, Kentucky. It flowed down the Muskingum, Little Kanawha, and Ohio Rivers and caught on fire. The blaze was spectacular, and many felt it to be a warning from God to leave things alone. The talk had barely died down when in 1820 near Pittsburgh, Pennsylvania, gas erupted from a salt well in the process of drilling, ignited, and burned down the salt factory.

Boston, Massachusetts, however, and New York City were not going to see their progress delayed by superstition and ignorance. Both (Boston in 1822, New York in 1823) chartered gas companies. In 1827, however, Berlin beat both New York and Boston to gas-lighted streets. It wasn't until 1828 that New Yorkers saw gas lights, on Broadway, between Grand Street and the Battery. The lights were so bright that Broadway became known as "the Great White Way." The gas lights went on in Boston on January 1, 1829.

In September of the next year there was an event of equal

significance. Down the rails of Liverpool & Manchester Rail Way Company in England came the locomotive *Rocket*, followed by seven other locomotives. The first trip ushered in the era of steam-powered railways. And in London, Marcus Samuel slipped anonymously into business as an importer of oriental goods, including fancy seashells. A hundred years later, the shell of the Shell Oil Company would be immediately recognized around the world.

In 1830, however, oil meant whale oil. The decade 1830–40 was both the golden age of whaling and the decade of whale slaughter, depending on whether you were a whaler or one of those who had the notion that the supply of whales actually was limited. Fortunes were made by successful whalers, whose vessels ranged the world in search of the largest mammal, and the oil to which its body could be reduced. Whale oil was selling for at least a dollar a gallon as the 1830s dawned, and the price rose steadily, both as the supply of whales diminished and the use of the whale oil increased. By 1840, whale oil averaged two dollars a gallon, and a decade later top quality whale oil brought five dollars.

The other major source of a fuel for illuminating lamps was the pine forests. By tapping pine trees, it was possible to make turpentine. From what we now think of as the "heavy end" (the less volatile) of turpentine it was possible to make, for sale at about a half a dollar a gallon, a substance called camphene. This liquid burned with a bright flame.

New Orleans chartered a gas-light company in 1832, but it was three years before the first gas lights were to flicker on in the Crescent City. In 1833 an English engineer named Hutchinson invented the telescopic gas holder. It's still with us, for in over 140 years no one has been able to improve on his idea for storing gas. The tanks, a familiar sight in any large city, are built of telescoping sections. As more gas is added to the tank, it extends like a telescope, and as gas is emptied, it retracts.

The next year, 1834, the city of Philadelphia built the first municipal gas works in America at 22d and Market Streets, right on the banks of the Schuykill River. Across the Delaware River from Philadelphia, the first American pipe foundry, making cast iron pipe for the Philadelphia Gas Works, started business. It took Philadelphia two years to get its plant built and the gas lines laid, and in 1836, with great fanfare, 19 private gas lamps were lit. Gas sold at $3.50 per 1,000 cubic feet.

England in the same year decided that the horseless carriage menace had gone far enough. Parliament passed laws requiring that all horseless carriages (which were railless steam locomotives) be preceded by a man on foot carrying a warning bell in the daytime and a lantern at night. And if that wasn't discouragement enough, Parliament levied prohibitive taxes in the form of tolls on non-horse-propelled vehicles using the public roads.

It has been suggested that these laws rank among Parliament's greatest blunders. England was then the center of the world's technology and manufacturing, the obvious place for the self-propelled vehicle industry to be born and be established. The Parliamentary decisions changed all that. The development of the self-propelled vehicle was taken over at first by the French, who experimented with it until the turn of the century. At that time the idea caught fire in America, which quickly became the most advanced (in terms of numbers and development) automotive nation in the world.

In 1837 an enterprising farmer near Findlay, Ohio, encountered natural gas while digging a water well. With a crude wooden pipe, most of it hollowed-out logs, he piped the gas to his house and then ran it through a discarded rifle barrel. The gas coming out the muzzle of the barrel was ignited, and he had heat and light absolutely free.

Then in 1840, in Butler County, Pennsylvania, salt maker John Criswell piped natural gas beneath his brine evaporation tanks and lit it. It was the first manufacturing use of gas in the United States. The word spread quickly, and in 1841 natural gas was being similarly used by William Thompkins in the Kanawha Valley of West Virginia.

Previously, coal (and sometimes even wood) had been used to boil the brine. Coal and wood had to be hauled to the steaming tables, and their ashes afterward had to be hauled away. Natural gas, once the pipes were in, eliminated the hauling, the shoveling, and the ash removal. While this was fine for the person who owned the factory, it was the reverse for the person who had been hauling the coal, wood, and ashes, since it put him out of a job. Resentment toward liquid or gaseous fuels with no residue, which continues today, was born simultaneously with the first use of gas as a commercial fuel.

On May 24, 1844, the first telegraph message was sent; it traveled from Washington to Baltimore. A month later in England a patent was issued to Robert Beart of Godmanchester for a rotary well-drilling machine. It had a rotating tool (cutter) and hollow drill rods and was designed so that it operated in a fluid (water at the time) which floated the cuttings out of the hole. It was very much like rotary drilling rigs in use today, the difference being one of refinement.

In Tarentum, Pennsylvania, the next year, the Hope Cotton Factory entered into a contract with Lewis Petersen, Sr., to provide the factory with two barrels of crude petroleum a week. It was used to replace sperm (whale) oil to lubricate the spindles in the mill. Sperm oil was $1.30 a gallon, oil was $.75.

The next year an Italian chemist, Professor Ascanio Sobrero, mixed nitric acid and glycerine together and came up with nitroglycerine. The same year the substance, modified slightly, was used successfully by Alfred Nobel in Sweden. Explosives became the basis of the Nobel fortune, and explosives (particularly nitroglycerine) developed into important tools in oil discovery and production.

In 1848, the year of the California Gold Rush, gas-light companies were organized in the nation's capitol and in Dayton, Ohio. Washington's gas came from oil, but Dayton decided to put to use the by-products of its slaughter houses. Animal fats were rendered into oil, and the oil was converted to gas. There is no record of what the gas works smelled like.

Coal was still the standard means of generating heat and power. In 1849 an Englishman named Edwards was granted a patent for a "gas-fire" which consisted of a gas burner under lumps of incombustible material. The lumps were heated to near incandescence, and the result, according to Edwards, "was virtually indistinguishable from a coal fire." Enterprising Americans resurrected Edwards's idea in the 1950s for the gas-charcoal stove, completing the circle.

The year 1850 was a big one for the growth of the petroleum industry. That year Chicago joined the ranks of illuminated cities. The city had 99 street lamps and 125 private customers for its Chicago Gas Light and Coke Company and charged the private consumers $3.00 per 1,000 cubic feet of gas.

In Ventura, California, oil from seepages was refined and used to illuminate several missions. In Pennsylvania, Samuel Kier, a druggist, canal-boat operator, and salt merchant, entered the oil business as a distiller, refining Pennsylvania crude into an illuminating oil he called "carbon oil." In Japan oil was first distilled, and in Oil Creek, Pennsylvania, two lumber mills (Brewer, Watson & Company and Hyde Brothers) were able to work their mills twenty-four-hours a day by using oil lamps for illumination.

But it wasn't until the next year, 1851, that the first oil lease in American history was signed. Dr. Francis Beattie entered into a contract with J. O. Angier of Titusville, Pennsylvania, for rights to the oil on Angier's land. Beattie wanted the oil for the lamps in his father's lumber mill.

In 1853 Emperor Franz-Ferdinand of Austria-Hungary lit the

oil lamps in Vienna's North Railway Station. Only the Austrians, grumbled other Europeans, would be so ostentatious. People who insisted on traveling at night should expect to do so in the dark.

The next year two partners, George H. Bissell and Jonathan G. Evelth, decided that there was money to be made producing oil for sale to others as a full-time occupation. They scraped together $5,000 and bought 105 acres of land in Venango County, Pennsylvania, with the announced purpose of "ditching for oil."

And ditch they did for two years, cutting shallow trenches across the land and waiting for oil to seep into the ditches. In 1856 Bissell came across an advertisement for Samuel Kier's carbon oil, which reported that he got his rock oil from depths of four hundred feet. Bissell inspected Kier's operation, and then Bissell and Evelth started looking for money for their own drilling.

Evelth apparently had second thoughts about the future of the business, for his name isn't found on the incorporation papers of the Pennsylvania Rock Oil Company of New York. The company was chartered in New York state, hence the odd name, and leased the Hibbard Farm near Titusville, Pennsylvania.

There was some friction almost immediately among the stockholders, most of it based on the inability of the company to start drilling for the oil that was going to make them all rich. The major stockholders formed a new company, the Seneca Oil Company, and hired Col. Edwin L. Drake to drill their first hole.

What inspired Bissell and the others was the rapid rise in wealth of Samuel M. Kier. Kier had been a perfectly ordinary Pittsburgh druggist and salt merchant. While drilling for salt water (the water was then evaporated and the remaining salt gathered for agricultural use) he'd struck oil. He found himself with a large quantity of a black substance for which he could think of no good use. He apparently had heard, however, of Phineas T. Barnum, who announced that a sucker was born every minute. And like Barnum, who always stretched the truth while seldom actually breaking it, Kier mixed the truth with his own opinion.

The label on Kier's rock oil was designed to look like a bank note. It was shaped like one, and it had 400 in each of its corners, as if it were a $400 bill. It also said the oil had been discovered in 1848 on the banks of the Allegheny River. The last part of that sentence was in large letters in type appropriate to the First National Bank of Chicago in the center of the label.

In A.D. 1849, the bill said, wonderful medical virtues were discovered. It didn't say these virtues had been found in Kier's Rock Oil, but if someone happened to get that idea, that was his problem. Kier's honesty was proven on the label, where he said bluntly that Kier's rock oil had come to the surface with salt water, had been stored in a cistern where it had risen to the surface, and had then been drawn off into barrels and "bottled in its natural state without any preparation or admixture."

In a brochure available separately to those who asked for it, however, Kier's rock oil was touted as the sure and only cure for every disease then known to medical science. It was equaled as a medication only by another miracle substance, given to humanity by God and Kier, which was intended to be rubbed on wounds and cuts, abrasions, rashes, pimples, sores, scratches, and other afflictions of the epidermis. This was Kier's petroleum butter, which was grease, pure and simple, and differed from bear grease only in that it had begun as petroleum.

George Bissell of New Haven, Connecticut, had been deeply affected by Kier's rock oil label. The label he saw was on a bottle sent to the chemists at Dartmouth College by a Titusville, Pennsylvania, physician who apparently questioned its all-around medical efficacy and wanted a scientific report on it before he prescribed it for his patients.

The chemists at Dartmouth hemmed and hawed and said little. Bissell said a good deal to his partner and they went off to Titusville and bought the farm. They leased an additional 112 acres north of town, and when they began to collect oil, they sent it off to Yale. Bissell suspected that he would get no more precise answer from the Yale chemists than the doctor had from the chemists at Dartmouth.

Professor Benjamin F. Stillman, Jr., reported back that while he could find very little to suggest that the oil would cure anything, it was possible to refine kerosene from it. Kerosene could probably be used in large amounts, Professor Stillman suggested, to light homes and even public buildings. Probably, the professor said, other uses could be found for it as time went on.

That was all that Bissell needed—confirmation from a respected member of the Yale faculty that there was something useful in that black stuff. The Pennsylvania Rock Oil and then the Seneca Oil companies were founded, the latter taking over the former's properties.

One of the most enthusiastic members of the Seneca organization was a banker. Instead of being opposed to any new idea that wasn't making money, James M. Townsend showed immediate enthusiasm. When Bissell told him that there was probably something to Kier's idea of drilling for oil as one drilled for salt water, rather than ditching for it, Townsend immediately agreed and said that they needed a professional well driller.

Townsend knew a retired railroad conductor by the name of Edwin Drake. The uniform he wore as a conductor was the only one Drake had ever worn, but he had drilled a couple of holes for water, and he had one other asset Townsend thought would come in handy. His retired status on the railroad gave him access to free passes for himself and his friends. That would solve the problem of how the officers of the Seneca Oil Company would get back and forth between New Haven and Pennsylvania at no charge.

Townsend decided, however, that retired railroad conductors didn't have quite as much status as, say, retired army colonels. He told Drake that henceforth he would be known as Colonel Drake. Drake thought that "Colonel Drake" had a nice ring to it and for the rest of his life referred to himself by that title.

Colonel Drake took the train to Corey, Pennsylvania, and there hired a horse and rode to the Seneca Oil Company property in Titusville. He quickly hired a man named Uncle Billy Smith, a toolmaker and blacksmith, and the two of them started drilling the first oil well.

The first rig was a very simple water well rig, of a type to which references can be found in the Bible. It consisted of a stout but elastic tree trunk cut off about six feet above the ground. The cut-off portion was then laid in the fork of another tree, and the base was tied to its original trunk at a right angle. On the narrow end of the pole, a tool (a shovel blade) was tied to the trunk, as were two foot stirrups. The tool was rammed into the earth by Drake and Uncle Billy. The elasticity of the tree trunk picked it back up, and then the drillers stepped on it again. Working all day, taking breaks only when at the brink of exhaustion, two good workers could drill as much as three feet a day.

The first oil well to be drilled in the United States was promptly dubbed "Drake's folly." Drake and Uncle Billy continued drilling. And then on Sunday afternoon, August 27, 1859, when the light was just right, Uncle Billy looked down into the hole (then 69.5 feet deep and lined with a stovepipe to keep the sides from falling in) and saw that the hole was filling with a black substance and that the top of the substance was just a few feet below the surface. America's first oil well had come in, and the course of the world had been changed.

chapter 3

PRODUCTION FROM COLONEL DRAKE'S WELL BE-
gan on August 28, 1859, and the word quickly spread that it
was producing 8, maybe as many as 10 barrels of oil a day.
Until August 27, 1859, the total oil production of the United
States was 2,000 barrels a year (as it was in the other major
producer, Russia). If that 10-barrel-a-day figure were true, that
meant Seneca Oil Company was going to produce almost 4,000
barrels a year from one well alone. Oil was worth $20 a barrel.

Before the month was over, everybody in the area was drunk
with ideas of becoming rich on oil. There was a frantic effort to
buy land, any land, in the valley, with buyers offering more
money for it than the original owners had ever seen. Then the
word spread farther. The owners of the Seneca Oil Company
were in New Haven, and they could not resist boasting of their
good fortune there. As a result, trainloads of would-be oil men
left New Haven for Corey, Pennsylvania, the nearest station to
Titusville. The trains passed through New York City on the way
and picked up an additional complement of New York investors.

The first of the big money men hit town and began to buy up
land from its new owners at prices beyond the second owners'
wildest dreams. At that point, there was a flash fire at Colonel

Drake's well, and the whole thing went up in flames. As soon as the flames were put out, the trading resumed.

One of the fascinated spectators was a nineteen-year-old native of the area, Lyman Stewart, whose original dream was to become a missionary and bring the word of God to the savages in far-off jungles. For the time being, he was engaged in the smelly business of leather tanning. His dedication to the missionary life, however, was not an idle fancy. He had saved $125 toward what he figured it would cost him to get the education necessary to become a missionary. In those days, $125 was an enormous amount of money for a young man to have.

When the oil fever hit Lyman Stewart in December 1859, he rationalized it by deciding that if he made a quick killing in the oil business, it would bring him that much closer to chasing Satan from the steaming jungles of Africa or Borneo.

He invested his $125 in a one-eighth interest in a lease on the farm of John Benninghoff, a Pennsylvania Dutch farmer. Benninghoff wasn't interested in any money he might get in the future. He wanted cash on the barrelhead for the right to drill for anything on his land—oil, salt, or water. When they paid Benninghoff, Lyman Stewart and his partners did so with the last of their capital. They couldn't raise the money to drill a well, the lease expired, and they were broke.

Benninghoff learned from the experience, too. He decided that he had been right to demand cash for the privilege of drilling for oil on his land. But he had been wrong, he realized, in leasing the whole thing. The next time some of these oil maniacs came to him about drilling rights, he would demand cash and a piece of the action. This was considered absolute heresy by the oil men, and Benninghoff didn't make another nickle from his land for six years. His neighbors, meanwhile, had grown rich (whether or not oil had been found) by selling the right to drill for oil on their lands.

Finally, in 1865, Benninghoff ran into oil drillers who would meet his terms. They paid him a large amount of money for drilling rights and in addition guaranteed him one-eighth of the profits, if any. No one remembers how much Benninghoff got for the initial rights to drill, for the well the second group of promoters drilled came in, and Benninghoff's one-eighth of the profits came to $6,000 a day.

It took Lyman Stewart until 1861 to save enough money for another try at the oil business. He had, for the moment, temporarily put aside his ambition of becoming a missionary. A number of other things happened in 1861. In January the first refinery was built in the Pennsylvania fields. It had 6 stills and bleachers and cost an awesome $15,000. In the same month 12 barrels of Pennsylvania oil, crude and refined, were sent to England to develop a market for it there.

In April the Confederate States of America were formed. Far more interesting to oil men was the well on the Buchanan Farm in Oil Creek, which came in on April 17 and actually flowed oil out of the ground at the rate of three thousand barrels a day. The same day it came in, it caught fire, set fire to the rest of the field, and cost nineteen people their lives. The fire and its tragic results weren't nearly as important to people as the idea that somewhere around Oil City, someone was going to find a flowing well that would flow oil at thousands of barrels a day.

There was so much oil, in fact, and the means to move it from the wells to the market were so inadequate, that for a time the price at the well head dropped to a dime a barrel.

It reached this low just after Lyman Stewart and his partners found oil on the Boyd farm. They had gone broke the first time because they hadn't had enough money to drill. They went broke the second time because they couldn't afford to pump oil from the well they drilled.

Shortly after they went broke again, the Oil Creek Association, consisting of most of the oil producers and landowners in the area, was formed. They refused to sell oil for less than four dollars a barrel. The boycott worked, and soon oil was flowing again.

In November the first shipload of petroleum was loaded aboard the schooner *Elizabeth Watts* in Philadelphia. She sailed with the tide, bound for London with 3,000 barrels of oil. The shipping rate was a dollar a barrel plus 5 percent of the proceeds.

Amazing things were happening in the oil fields in addition to the antics of the oil promoters. When the oil came out of the ground, either by pumping or by flowing, no one really knew what to do with it. The immediate solution was to scrape out little depressions in the earth and establish oil lakes. There were several problems with this, among them the fact that the oil which did not seep right back into the ground had a tendency to give off vapors, which then ignited.

The best solution, of course, was to put the oil in barrels. But barrels were expensive, and their price increased with the demand. Next came the idea of storing oil in wooden boxes. Building boxes required less skill and lower quality lumber than did barrels, and, since the oil was free to begin with, no one really cared about a little leakage.

The barrel-sized wooden boxes led naturally to wooden storage areas, boarded-in square holes in the ground. So long as drillers took the trouble to dig a hole to surround the huge wooden boxes, that was a good solution. But soon digging a hole seemed too much trouble, and square tanks were built above ground. A number of them, filled with oil, suddenly groaned, creaked, and burst, sending small floods of oil all over the surrounding land.

Then a man named Akin built a device at Titusville which seemed to be the answer. First he laid a floor of wood. Then he built a round wooden structure on it and looped bands of iron around it. The round tanks held as much as 12 barrels of oil (504 gallons), and soon they were as much in evidence around

Oil Creek as mushrooms had been before Colonel Drake arrived.

Railroad workers labored frantically to build a double-track
line from Corey into Titusville, but in the meantime Oil Creek
itself was put to use. In the spring there was enough water in Oil
Creek to float barges, but it was also shallow enough so that
horses could pull the barges through the water.

Soon there was a steady stream of barrel-laden barges moving
from Titusville to the Allegheny River and back again. As soon
as the empty barrels reached the oil fields, they were filled with
oil, sealed, and loaded back on the barges. Steamboats on the
Allegheny carried the barrels to market, first entirely by water,
then by rail, and eventually by rail in the first tank cars, which
were made up from regular flat cars equipped with two of the
round, banded tanks invented by Akin.

What was happening in the oil business soured Lyman Stewart. He had lost his chance to become a missionary, and he had
now gone broke twice, through bad luck and ignorance, as an
oil man. Perhaps he would be able to find himself in the service;
perhaps military glory would come to him in the Civil War. He
enlisted as a private in the 16th Pennsylvania Volunteer Cavalry
in September 1862. Three years later Private Lyman Stewart
returned to the oil fields. He had been something less than a
spectacular soldier, too.

Lyman Stewart learned that a great deal had happened while
he had been at war. He found out that Belgium alone had taken
1,500,000 gallons of petroleum, all of it from the Pennsylvania
fields, during 1862. In 1863 the Pennsylvania legislature passed
the first antipollution bill, forbidding the running of tar and
other distillery refuse into certain creeks. Disposing of refuse
and rock material from the drilling site had been a continuing
problem. A patent was issued to J. R. Leschot for a drilling rig
which used both a diamond-surfaced cutting tool (to cut
through rock) and "mud," a liquid flushing system, to get the

loosened material from the bottom of the hole. The hole was flooded by a mixture of dirt and water spouting out at the drill bit. As it filled the hole and flooded over, it carried away the material the bit had chopped loose as it drilled. The consistency of the "mud" was and is a matter of judgment. Water alone wouldn't lift stone chips, and too thick a dirt-and-water mixture wouldn't flow out of the hole. Today, the "mudman" (a practicing physicist dealing with fluid dynamics) is a highly respectable and highly paid oil field professional, despite his undignified title, which has gone unchanged for over a century.

Oil had been discovered in other places than around Oil Creek, and as soon as it had been found, so had markets for it. Oil from Canada, for example, was being shipped in iron tanks on railroad flatcars to Portland, Maine, and then was sent by sea to Liverpool, England. The Russians opened their first refinery in the Baku fields that same year, and in Boston, Massachusetts, a man named Joshua Merrill began the first commercial production of gasoline. Most people couldn't understand that, as no one so far had found any use for gasoline. The federal government was talking about stationing an inspector at refineries to make sure that unscrupulous and dishonest distillers didn't slip any gasoline into the kerosene they were making.

The most important thing to happen in the oil business in 1863, however, went practically unnoticed. Two men, partners in a mercantile commission house (people sent them things to sell for a percentage), Maurice B. Clark and John D. Rockefeller went into partnership with a man named Samuel Andrews to manufacture kerosene.

The next year saw even more spectacular developments. One involved Lyman Stewart's childhood schoolmate, John Washington Steele. Johnny Steele started life with two strikes against him. His parents died when he was a child, and he lived on the charity of his neighbors until he was in his teens. He was then adopted by Mr. and Mrs. Culbertson McClintock, who gave him the home he had never had before. Shortly after oil was found on the McClintock property, Mr. McClintock died. Johnny Steele proved a dutiful son to his adopted mother, and when she died in early 1864, she left her entire property to him.

The income from the property was two thousand dollars a day. Johnny Steele decided that it was time to make up for the poverty and deprivation of his youth, so he went to New York. In a year he was back, flat broke. In that year he had managed to spend not only the two thousand dollar a day income on himself and an army of parasites, but all the money he got for the sale of the property itself. When Lyman Stewart returned to the oil fields, Johnny Steele was already working at the job he held for the rest of his life, baggage handler at the railway depot, for about a dollar a day, plus tips. Steele's record as the world's greatest spendthrift has never been equaled.

And the prices of oil property along Oil Creek continued to rise. A record price of $650,000 in cash for a farm along Oil Creek set in April lasted only until November, when $750,000 in greenbacks changed hands for another Oil Creek farm.

Everybody was getting into the act, including a member of a distinguished family of actors, John Wilkes Booth. Booth and two others formed the Dramatic Oil Company to drill for oil near Franklin, Pennsylvania. Six weeks after Booth shot President Abraham Lincoln in Ford's Theatre in Washington, his well came in. It was a gusher.

The government got in the act, too, with a tax of one dollar per barrel of crude oil. The howls of protest from oil men could be heard for miles, and more cash in suitcases headed for Washington. It took them until December of the next year to apply sufficient grease to the proper wheels, but the tax was finally lifted.

And new uses for oil kept appearing. J. K. Wright, a Philadelphia ink maker, directed an oil-gas flame at a slowly revolving steel plate. Carbon accumulated on the plate and was scraped off by a knife as the plate revolved. The carbon was then mixed with grease, and a new source of ink, far cheaper than anything previously developed, was found. The same principle is still used in making ink.

The navy announced that it was considering the use of oil as fuel for men-of-war. It had heard that a Hudson River steamboat had been successfully using gas to light its lamps for a year, which seemed to disprove the theory that whenever oil was used aboard a ship, an explosion was sure to follow.

In the oil fields a man named Frederick Crocker wondered why some oil fields flowed (indeed, some literally gushed) while others just seeped. He wondered what would happen if he caused an explosion at the bottom of a slow-flowing oil well, an explosion large enough to crack the subsurface rock and sand formations. He made up a torpedo, consisting of a package of gunpowder (black powder) narrow enough to fit down the pipe. He detonated it by putting a pistol cartridge in the explosive primer end up and then dropping a weight down the hole. The cartridge fired, detonating the black powder, and the explosion caused a greatly increased flow of oil.

In January 1865 Col. E. L. Roberts (also self-appointed; following the successful "Colonel" Drake, the oil fields commissioned just about as many colonels as the army had during the Civil War) for the first time used nitroglycerine to shoot a well. Nitroglycerine, which was about thirteen times as powerful as black powder, had a number of advantages over black powder in application. For one thing, it possessed the power to crack a rock strata which black powder didn't always have. For another, oil men had learned that oil-bearing strata were often quite thin, as thin as several feet. A three-foot long section of explosive charge of black powder often wouldn't crack a strata. A three-foot section of nitroglycerine was thirteen times more powerful and did the job. The use of nitroglycerine quickly introduced a new specialist to the oil fields, the "nitro man," of whom it was said he had a highly paid, if often short, career. His descendants remain among the aristocrats of the oil-field technicians.

In September 1865 the first true tank car left the oil fields of Pennsylvania for New York. It had been designed and built by Amos Densmore for the specific purpose of hauling oil and carried two tanks, each holding about forty-five barrels. But already people were saying that moving oil on wheels was not the answer to land transportation of petroleum. The very next month another new idea was put to the test.

The Oil Transportation Association laid 32,000 feet (about 6 miles) of 2-inch iron pipe from a well to the Miller's Farm station of the Oil Creek Railroad. On October 16 it went into service, pumping 80 barrels an hour. This was as much oil as 300 teamsters and their 1,200 horses could move in the standard 10-hour working day. While the Oil Transportation Association patted itself on the back, the teamsters began to plot how they could defeat this threat to their trade.

In California, meanwhile, drawn there by tales of seepage much like those told of Oil City in the days before Colonel Drake, Thomas A. Bard put down his first well in July 1865 on the Rancho Ojai, north of San Buenaventura. He found some oil, but his first hole produced far more water.

In the Pennsylvania fields, oil refiner Charles Pratt who was concerned with selling his product (mostly kerosene) in the small amounts that the retail customer would want, decided that there had to be a middle way between the forty-two- or fifty-five-gallon drum and the one-gallon pottery jug. He hired a German, Herman Miller, to invent something better. Miller came up with an oblong can that was square on top and made of tin-plated thin sheet steel. It held five gallons and was an immediate success. As the standard vessel for transporting kerosene (and later gasoline) it lasted until World War II, when an unknown German invented a can of stamped steel with a self-contained handle and greater strength and durability. It was called the "jerry can" by the Western Allies, who were quick to recognize its superiority and adopt it for their own armed forces.

In 1865 a man named Charles Cheseborough divided his time between his laboratory, his law office, and the United States Patent Office. When he was through, in 1866, he had patents covering just about every way of filtering coal oil or petroleum through charcoal, bone-black, or other material, whether the petroleum was hot or cold, whether it was under pressure or not, and whether or not the filter was heated. One of his processes produced what we now call Vaseline, the bedrock of the Cheseborough-Ponds Company.

And as 1865 drew to a close, John D. Rockefeller went into partnership with Samuel Andrews and bought out his old partner Maurice B. Clark's interest in their refinery. The new firm was called Rockefeller & Andrews.

chapter 4

LYMAN STEWART, HIS DREAMS OF MISSIONARY glory, oil glory, and finally military glory all having disappeared, came out of the army with enough money to last him about six months.

He went to Poughkeepsie, New York, and enrolled in Eastman's Business College. By the time his money had run out, he had completed courses in bookkeeping and what was probably the theory of finance, but little else. While he was still deeply religious (he carried a Bible in his pocket during and after the Civil War), he had abandoned once and for all the idea of becoming a missionary.

But he had not given up the idea of going into the oil business. Armed with his diploma from Eastman's Business College, he returned to the oil fields of Pennsylvania and opened an office through which, he announced, he would conduct the business of negotiating oil leases.

"Opened an office" sounds far more elegant and substantial than was the case. His office was no more than a desk in a corner of a small room in what could be described as a shack. He couldn't afford the rent of similar accommodations in Titusville and set up business in the little village of Pioneer Run, a few miles away. Titusville was now bustling with a population of at least six thousand people, and it was impossible to get a room in any of the seven hotels which had sprung up. There were three and four beds to a room and two men to a bed.

Stewart had one asset few others in the area had. When he had been apprenticed as a leather tanner, his duties had sent him traveling all over the area when it was still farmland, his wagon loaded with hides from the farmers for the tannery. He had spent countless hours ambling along in a horse-drawn wagon with nothing to do but examine the scenery. He knew where the "seeps" had been, and he knew where there had been no indication of oil. He also had twice come to grief in the oil business for not knowing what he was up to, and he vowed that wasn't going to happen again. And this time, things looked promising.

Almost as soon as he'd hired desk space and announced he was in business, a wildcat well near Pioneer Run came in producing six hundred barrels a day. The promoters, speculators, drillers, and financiers began to move in the next day. The farmers in the area were either Pennsylvania Dutch or Scotch-Irish or a mixture of the two. Before long they realized that Rule One in dealing with oil people was absolute distrust.

Lyman Stewart, on the other hand, was one of their own. Long before oil had been anything but a smelly nuisance in the area, Lyman had been there. He was a hard-working, God-fearing, church-going poor man just like they were. When Lyman Stewart told a farmer that he thought so much money was all a lease on his land was worth, the farmer was willing to take his word.

Lyman Stewart quickly prospered after that first Pioneer Run wildcat. Having been burned twice, he took his profits from a percentage of the money that actually changed hands, rather than from a percentage of the wells and their production. This was a sound decision on his part, too.

After the first wildcat came in, another gushed in at Pit Hole, producing two hundred fifty barrels a day. More wells were

sunk, and soon the field was producing about six thousand barrels a day. Drilling rigs stood side by side, and a town, sprouting
drilling derricks as other towns had trees, sprang up with them.
It grew to have a population of fifteen thousand, the third largest
post office in Pennsylvania, and a row of crude frame buildings
which served as hotels, banks, and saloons.

And then, one by one, the wells stopped producing. Almost as
quickly as it had sprung up, the town of Pit Hole died. It was an
Eastern ghost town. But this time when the boom broke, Lyman
Stewart and his brother Milton, with whom he had formed a
loose partnership, were not broke.

Demand for oil continued to rise as new uses for it were
found. In 1867 the Franklin & Warren Railroad successfully
tested oil to fire the boilers of its locomotives. The month before,
the navy had steamed the gunboat U.S.S. *Palos* for 25 nautical
miles at the remarkable speed of 14 knots. That kind of speed
had been possible under coal, but only for short bursts, because
people couldn't shovel coal into boilers fast enough. The navy
report spelled it out clearly: 4 barrels of oil had carried the *Palos*
as far as 7 or 8 tons of coal would have carried it and had moved
the *Palos* over the 25 nautical miles 50 percent faster than
would have been possible with coal. The other advantages were
obvious: with bunkers filled with oil, rather than coal, 4 or 5 or
10 times as much fuel could be carried.

The navy in those days was establishing coaling stations
around the world as it became obvious that the days of the
sailing vessel were numbered. Coal was either procured locally
or brought by ship at enormous expense to be stockpiled against
future need. If oil could be used in place of coal, particularly if
fuel had to be transported to a fueling station, the cost of transportation would be greatly reduced and so would the cost of
storage.

But the most significant development in science affecting the
oil business went practically unnoticed. Near Mannheim, Ger-

many, Nikolaus August Otto and Eugen Langen built what they called the Otto Silent Gas Engine. It wasn't silent; it wasn't very efficient; and it wasn't very powerful (about one horsepower), but it was the first successful internal combustion engine.

Until the Otto Silent Gas Engine was built, there had been only the steam engine. This worked by heating water and converting it to steam, which would then push a piston. Otto's engine eliminated the water and the steam. He used the force generated by the burning of petroleum gases inside the cylinder to move the piston.

Rockefeller was making a few moves, too. In 1867, he announced that in "order to unite skill and capital in order to carry on a business of some magnitude and importance" firms in which he had an interest (Rockefeller, Andrews & Flagler, Rockefeller & Andrews, and Rockefeller & Company) would merge with William Rockefeller & Company, S. V. Harkness, and H. M. Flagler. What Rockefeller had in mind was controlling the entire petroleum industry, but he kept that intention to himself.

The first of the oil storage tanks resembling those that cover the world today was built at Bellow's Island, New York, in 1867 by Eghest & Brown. It was a monster: twenty-two feet three inches tall, with a diameter of eighty feet. Even before it was finished, plans were announced to build another.

Lyman Stewart, meanwhile, continued to prosper in the Pennsylvania oil fields. He kept up his brokerage business and moved back into investing in wells themselves. The early oil men felt far more comfortable with fractions than percentages. Corporations to search and drill for wells were formed by offering prospective investors the chance to invest half the money in exchange for half the profits. If half seemed like too large a piece, then people invested in quarters, then eights, sixteenths, thirty-seconds, sixty-fourths, one-twenty-eights, and even two-fifty-sixths.

It soon made sense to most investors to split their investments (or, more accurately, gambles), as far as possible; in other words, it was better to own an eighth of four different wells than it was to own half of just one well. A person doing that had four chances that a well would come in, instead of just one.

This practice, splitting an oil venture into tiny fractions, exists today in the oil business. But today, there are laws which specifically prohibit, under heavy penalties, the practice of selling more fractions than add up to the whole.

In the early days, however, unscrupulous promoters figured that since most wells didn't come in anyway, those twenty or thirty people to whom they had sold sixteenth interests would never know the difference. If the hole did come in, the problem could then be handled, most often by leaving town and permitting the shareholders to fight over the profits.

Lyman Stewart and his brother Milton always made sure when they bought a sixteenth-interest in a well that only fifteen other sixteenths would be sold. They owned small interests (generally sixteenths) in several hundred wells, and Milton had gone into the refinery business. Lyman Stewart formed the Lyman Stewart Company, and stock was issued to himself, Milton, another brother, two sisters, a cousin, a friend, and a Presbyterian minister.

He married on May 2, 1867, and later built a house. He soon became a legend in the oil business, not only because of his business acumen, but also because he played the role of Christian gentleman in the fields. In a time and place where profanity approached the status of a fine art, Lyman Stewart was known as the man who never swore at all. Not one irreverent, risqué, or even colorful word passed his lips. Furthermore, he insisted on making his rounds through the muck and mire of the fields in immaculate, often white, clothing, fastidiously barbered and reeking of gentlemen's cologne.

Culture, too, entered his life and saw him go broke again. The

Titusville Mendelssohn Society was the private preserve of respectable oil men, dedicated to the cultural enrichment of the oil
fields. Lyman Stewart was a driving force in the society and a
regular participant at its affairs.

But one night, en route to a meeting of the society, he permitted commerce to interfere with his obligations to culture. A
man came to town with what looked like a fascinating proposal
to get richer quicker than was possible even in the oil business.
Lyman Stewart went off to discuss with him the financial possibilities of the agricultural implement business.

Milton Stewart went to the Mendelssohn Society Meeting.
After an evening rich in culture, he and some friends formed the
Octave Oil Company, the name a tribute to the musical char-
acter of the evening. Octave put down some wells; they came in;
and everybody made money.

Lyman Stewart, however, whose income was then about a
thousand dollars a week, who had about a quarter of a million
dollars in cash, decided that he could well afford a small commercial venture in farm implements. He was so convinced that it
was a sure thing that he talked Milton into coming in with him.

On the surface, it seemed like a good business proposition.
Every farmer needed a better mowing machine than those presently available. Stockholders in a firm which manufactured one,
were sure to reap large profits. Unfortunately, the mowing
machine didn't work, and the man promoting it was a crook.
After running up large debts in the Stewart brothers' name for
supplies and equipment which he promptly sold, putting the
money in his pocket, he vanished.

By the time Lyman and Milton became aware of what had
happened, they had not only gone through all the money they
had in the bank, but they were forced to sell off their hundreds
of oil properties to pay the bills that remained. It wasn't the first
time that a sharp operator had clipped a man with oil money,
but it was one of the longest swindles on record and one of the

few which took as suckers men with a high position in the industry.

Stewart was back where he started, except that he now had a wife and family. He had been making a thousand dollars a week, and now, to put food on the table, he went to work at a salary of about thirty dollars a week.

In May 1869 a golden spike was hammered into the ground at Promontory Point, Utah, and the United States was banded together by the steel rails of the transcontinental railroad. And halfway across the world the Suez Canal was opened, permitting transit from Europe and England through the Mediterranean to Asia and eliminating the necessity of sailing around Africa. On January 10, 1870, a new firm was chartered in Cleveland, Ohio. It absorbed the Rockefeller interests and took John D. Rockefeller, by far the majority stockholder in the million-dollar corporation, one step closer to control of the petroleum industry.

In May of the same year, the brand new (and still standing) city hall of Newark, New Jersey, had one more marvel in an array of latest developments of which to boast. The street in front of the city hall was paved with asphalt, the city fathers hailing it as a milestone in the progress of humanity. Apparently, no one told them that asphalt had been used as a paving material long before Europe had been civilized. But it was the first such paving in the United States.

That same month, the S.S. *Charles* sailed from New York harbor carrying 794 tons of oil. The *Charles* was the first vessel fitted for the bulk shipment of oil and had converted its holds to carry (in 59 tanks) nothing but oil. In Hoboken, New Jersey, Stevens Institute opened its doors for the first time. Over the years Stevens has produced a disproportionate number of scientists and engineers (and, for that matter, executives who began as scientists and engineers) for the oil industry.

The big news of 1871 had a tenuous petroleum connection. A cow owned by a Mrs. O'Leary in Chicago kicked over a kerosene lamp, and the resulting fire nearly destroyed Chicago. More than 18,000 buildings in a 1,688-acre area burned to the ground. In the same year an oil tank car resembling modern tank cars first rolled down the rails. It was made up of a horizontal cylindrical tank and mounted on two four-wheeled platforms (trucks). The only changes since have been improvements in the trucks (primarily tapered bearings), in filling and emptying valves and fittings, and, of course, in size.

In 1872 there were the opening rounds of oil business warfare, echoes of which can still be heard. On January 18, 1872, the Pennsylvania, New York Central, and Erie Railroads signed a contract with the South Improvement Company granting the company rebates on all petroleum products carried by them. The South Improvement Company had nothing to do with the South or anybody named South, and the only thing it was interested in improving was the bank balance of the people who owned the company.

It had made a deal, quite openly, with the railroads, which provided for the payment of a certain percentage of transportation costs by the railroads back to the shippers. Only the members of the improvement company would get the repayment, or rebate, which meant that their oil or petroleum products would cost less at the final destination than the products of people who had to pay the full fare.

On the other side in the battle was the Petroleum Producers Association. It promptly enacted an embargo on crude oil shipments of any kind. On March 25, the railroads gave in and publicly abrogated their contract with South Improvement Company. A week later, the Pennsylvania legislature revoked the charter of the South Improvement Company with one rap of the gavel and then with the next rap passed a free pipeline bill, giving pipelines the same right of eminent domain the railroads enjoyed.

Eminent domain is the legal principle that the right of the

whole society in anyone's property is more substantial than the individual right. In other words, if society will be better served by running a railroad or a highway or a pipeline across somebody's front lawn, the owner has to sell his front lawn for that purpose, whether he wants to or not.

The railroads had long enjoyed the right of eminent domain. State legislatures and the federal government had decided that railroads were a good thing and that they should have precedence over individual rights. Now the legislature of Pennsylvania decided that an oil pipeline was similar. Since the pipeline would serve all the people, the oil company should also have the right to buy what property it needed for it, whether or not the owner wanted to sell it.

In the same month the oil industry finally decided how many gallons went into a barrel of oil. After heated argument it was decided that a barrel contained forty-two gallons, no more and no less. It wasn't until 1916 (forty-two years later) that the United States Congress made this official.

In August John D. Rockefeller was elected president of the newly formed Petroleum Refiners Association (also known as the National Refiners Association). In December the association signed an agreement by which it would buy crude oil from the Petroleum Producers Agency. It was called "the Treaty of Titusville."

The agreement was quite out in the open, but it contained certain shady possibilities. So long as the two groups (producers and refiners) were separate, it was a fine idea that the producers should determine the price of the crude oil they would sell the refiners.

There was nothing in the agreement that said that a refiner could not be a producer, too, and that was the snake in the woodpile. Gradually, producers who were also refiners began to gain the power in the producers association to sell crude oil at a price satisfactory to the refiners. Once the refiner-producers assumed control of the producers association, the refiners actually set the price of crude, and the other producers were obliged by contract to go along. None of this happened overnight. The men who were determined to control the petroleum industry were clever, patient, and cautious. But gradually, the net tightened.

The industry grew rapidly (petroleum was now the fifth or sixth most valuable product exported from the United States) in 1873 and 1874. In 1875 the Central Refiners Association was formed. To nobody's surprise, the president was John D. Rockefeller.

Robert Magee Downie of Butler, Pennsylvania, had decided that an important, rapidly growing industry like oil, should have some better way of getting at its raw material than by slamming a bit into the earth at the end of a spring pole, as Colonel Drake had done on the first well. He sat down at his drawing board and came up with a startling innovation. He didn't get it built until 1878, but it was welcomed eagerly. Instead of having two or more men slam the bit into the ground, he hooked it to a steam engine.

On November 22, 1878, the Tidewater Pipe Company, Ltd., completed a 110-mile pipeline from the oil fields over the mountains to the Philadelphia and Reading Railroad depot at Williamsport, Pennsylvania. Everybody but John D. Rockefeller, who until the line began pumping 10,000 barrels a day had controlled virtually all the oil shipped from the fields by rail, was happy. Sixty-five percent of all American oil production was being exported, and 80 to 90 percent of that export consisted of illuminating oil or kerosene.

In Titusville, meanwhile, the fortunes of Lyman Stewart were looking up, even if he wasn't back in the thousand-dollar-a-week category. When he had money, he had gone out of his way to help a trio of brothers, James, Harvey, and Wallace Hardison, who were also farm boys suddenly thrust into the oil business.

James and Harvey started out as drillers, and Wallace had

gone out west to cut ties for the railroad. They were Stewarts' kind of people—hard-working, anyway, if not quite so pure of speech, dress, or deportment. When James and Harvey needed money to get their drilling business going, Stewart had loaned it to them.

About 1878 Wallace came back from the West, where he'd made a fortune with railroad ties. He had been impressed with the dignified Mr. Lyman Stewart; and with his pockets now full, he returned to the oil fields with a dignity he hoped would match that of Mr. Stewart.

He found that Mr. Stewart had fallen on hard times and was working for thirty dollars a week. Mr. Hardison proposed to Mr. Stewart that they enter the oil business together. Mr. Stewart told Mr. Hardison that while he would be honored to enter into a business relationship with Mr. Hardison, he must regretfully decline because he did not possess the necessary financial resources.

Mr. Hardison told Mr. Stewart that if Mr. Stewart would be good enough to contribute his knowledge of the petroleum industry to a joint venture, he would be delighted to provide the necessary financial support. Mr. Stewart and Mr. Hardison (who never, despite their long subsequent years of association, involving many millions of dollars, stopped calling each other "mister" or addressing one another in what they regarded as proper language for gentlemen) shook hands, and Stewart was almost instantly back in the oil business.

Stewart had another friend from his oil days, Capt. J. T. Jones, the largest producer in the newly discovered Bradford oil fields. In Stewart's own words: "It looked like a good proposition to me, as I had thus far made but little progress toward regaining the ground lost by failure" (of the agricultural implement business). Stewart and Hardison rode to Bradford, Stewart looked over the land, Hardison came up with the money, and they leased some of Jones's land. The wells they put down came in, but, while they prospered, there was not the instant fortune of earlier times.

The big operators, in particular the groups headed by Rockefeller, controlled the distribution facilities. They also controlled the railroads, the exchanges, and the markets. Oil which had been worth two dollars and more a gallon at the well head was down to eight cents, less than the cost of pumping it.

Hardison and Stewart realized they couldn't take on Rockefeller and sold out. Stewart sat on his money for a while, and Hardison used his to get elected to the Pennsylvania legislature. While he was in Harrisburg, he exerted all of his considerable influence to get a law passed which cut into Rockefeller and the others. He had pipelines declared common carriers. This meant that they had to pump anyone's oil who was willing to pay the charge, and it meant that the charge was if not set by the legislature, then controlled by it. If a pipeline company pumped so much of Rockefeller's oil for ten dollars, then it had to pump exactly that much oil for anyone else with ten dollars.

Once he'd accomplished that, Mr. Hardison shook hands with Mr. Stewart and took the train to Kansas. Mr. Stewart thought the grass looked even greener in southern California and in 1883, leaving his wife behind him, he set out for California with about fifty thousand dollars in cash and a Bible.

"What I was to find in the West, I knew not," he said many years later, "except that it was an opportunity, and that was all I asked. With me I carried a small Bible Mrs. Stewart had given me many years before. That Bible was to be my guide and protector, my inspiration during the hectic and discouraging times ahead."

chapter 5

IN CALIFORNIA IN 1880 THE STANDARD OIL COM-
pany of California built a 500-barrel-a-day refinery at Alameda
and laid the first pipe line, 5 miles long and 2 inches in diameter,
between Pico and Newhall. Col. Edwin L. Drake died on November 8, 1880, at Bethlehem, Pennsylvania. He would have died
broke, except that the Pennsylvania legislature, in a rare case
of recognizing a person's contribution before his death, had
voted him a life-long pension.

On January 1, 1881, it was announced that, since August
27, 1859, when Drake had brought in the first well, Pennsylvania
had produced 156,890,931 barrels of oil—95 percent of the
total United States production.

In January 1882 a new kind of business arrangement came
into being with the signing of the Standard Oil trust agreement.
The stock of twenty-nine separate oil companies was placed,
"for safe keeping and management," in the hands of nine "trus-
tees" who would manage the affairs of all the companies. It had
a nice, respectable ring to it. But what the Standard Oil trust
meant was the complete domination of the oil business in the
United States and around the world. The head trustee was John
D. Rockefeller, and under his direction the Standard Oil trust
began to establish control of petroleum from the moment some-

one suspected it lay under his land until the moment the final retail customer bought a quart of kerosene for his lamp.

The same year a Dutchman named Aeilco Janz Zijlker returned to Holland from Sumatra to try to borrow enough money to get into the oil business himself. Two years before Zijlker had been superintendent of a tobacco plantation on the east coast of Sumatra. While he was making the rounds of his plantation, a storm had forced him to take refuge in a drying barn. His native guide set fire to a torch to provide light. The torch burned with brilliance and little smoke.

Zijlker was fascinated, for most native torches burned with a dull glow and a good deal of black smoke. The guide told him that for years people in the area had been making torches by rubbing them with "earthwax." Earthwax was a substance skimmed from the surface of certain small pools of water in the area.

The next morning Zijlker was shown some of the pools. They reeked with the unmistakable odor of kerosene, a substance which even then was being shipped to the Dutch East Indies by an enterprising Pennsylvania merchant named John D. Rockefeller.

Zijlker took some samples of the fluid to Batavia, where a chemist informed him that it would indeed make very fine lamp oil, of a quality to match or excell Rockefeller's kerosene, and that a simple refining process would get six gallons of kerosene out of every ten gallons of the fluid. The earthwax with which the natives rubbed their torches was the residue of the petroleum which had naturally evaporated in the air; nature had itself been the refinery.

Zijlker went to the sultan of Langkat, who reigned over the area (under the authority of the Dutch) and got a lease to explore for and produce petroleum. Then he went to the local banks and tried to raise some money. They advanced him several thousand dollars (in Dutch guilders) for his immediate expenses and suggested that he go home to Holland to raise the large amounts of money it would take to look for oil and build the necessary tank and pipeline facilities he would need should he find it.

The Dutch bankers weren't at all receptive. They didn't believe that there could be oil in the Dutch East Indies, and they didn't like the terms of the lease Zijlker had obtained from the sultan. No money was forthcoming, and Zijlker returned to Sumatra. First, he obtained a better lease (to run for seventy-five years, encompassing a vast area known as the Telega Said tract) from the sultan, and then, with local money, he started to drill.

In June 1885 the second well drilled (Telega Toenggal No. 1) came in at seventy-two feet (three feet deeper than Drake's first well in Pennsylvania) and began to produce oil, but only about five barrels a day. That was hardly enough to make it worthwhile to start refineries and distribution systems, and everybody involved in the operation, except Zijlker, became discouraged. Rockefeller's kerosene continued to burn in Sumatra's lamps.

In the same year two Germans were at work on ideas that would increase the demand for petroleum beyond anyone's comprehension. Gottlieb Daimler succeeded that year in developing an internal combustion engine which ran on "lighter vapors" of petroleum (gasoline) and was small enough to be mounted on a bicycle. It became, of course, the first motorcycle. And in Munich a three-wheeled vehicle powered by a one-cylinder gasoline engine was driven around by its inventor, Karl Benz. The next year, he added a fourth wheel.

Lyman Stewart and his partner Wallace Hardison (who had left Kansas to join Stewart) weren't doing very well. Soon after arriving in California, Stewart looked into the Pico Canyon Area, decided there would be oil under the ground, and wired Hardison, back in Pennsylvania, to that effect.

D. J. Swartz (left) and Hal Proudfoot, Pennsylvania oil men brought west by Hardison and Stewart, standing by the Hardison and Stewart rig at Tar Creek, California, in 1888. UNION OIL PHOTO.

Hardison's reply had been simple. All his telegram gave was the date of his arrival in California. He didn't even tell his partner that he had bought two of the heaviest available drilling rigs or that he had recruited two experienced crews, thirty-five men in all, to run them and had guaranteed them six months' wages.

They started to work as soon as they arrived in California. The first hole was dry, and the second. The third, fourth, fifth, sixth, and seventh holes were dry, too. They ran through their capital (about $135,000) and were $183,000 in debt.

They moved farther into the canyon and started drilling Star No. 1 well. At 1,620 feet it came in, but it wasn't a gusher. Even with a pump production was no more than 75 barrels a day. They felt that they had hit oil on the edge of a pool, but when they tried to lease more land to drill another well, one which they hoped would gush, the California Star Oil Company refused to lease it to them. The company, aware of Stewart and Hardison's financial problems, also pressured them into selling the Star No. 1 well to them.

"Discouraged but undaunted," in Stewart's own words, they moved to Adams Canyon and put down Adams No. 1. They struck oil, and their enthusiasm soared. Their streak of bad luck was over. This seemed to be proved when Adams No. 2 came in. But when they started to pump from Adams No. 2, the oil was drained from Adams No. 1. Adams No. 3 went down, struck oil, and again, when the pump was put to the well, production stopped at Adams No. 2.

In all of 1884 Stewart and Hardison produced only 2,661 barrels of oil, which, selling for $2.50 a barrel, didn't even pay the drilling crews, much less the cost of equipment.

The year 1885 wasn't much better. Total sales amounted to 4,806 barrels of oil, but in that year Stewart put his mind to the question of reducing production and drilling costs and developed the revolutionary idea of using crude oil from the oil field to fire the steam engines. The engines were using coal as fuel, even though coal dealers charged $30 a ton for coal delivered to the oil fields. Even at that price coal was cheaper than using refinery-processed crude oil would have been.

No one challenged the established system: crude oil could not be used as a fuel because of the difficulty of getting it to burn steadily. It had never been done before, and therefore, everyone said, it could not be done.

Stewart didn't accept that line of reasoning. He and his tool machinists set to work to make it possible. The first idea was simplicity itself. Crude oil was dripped onto a bed of rocks in the furnace of the steam engine. That didn't work. Either it didn't generate enough heat, or it flared up and set the dripping pipe on fire. The next idea was a bellows which blew the oil in a spray into the boiler. This worked, on and off, because the crude would sometimes spray, sometimes come out in a stream, and sometimes clog the spray nozzle. Finally, Stewart's machinists came up with a pump which fed a steady, small stream of crude oil into the firebox.

That worked. Not only did it put the coal merchants completely out of business in the oil fields within a couple of months, but, because so much power was required in the oil fields, it doubled the local market for oil.

Stewart then turned his attention to the problem of transportation. His market for oil was San Francisco; his production facilities were in Santa Paula. The railroads were charging $1.00 a barrel to ship oil to San Francisco. (Some oil was also going out of a tiny port in southern California called Los Angeles). It pained Lyman Stewart deeply to pay the railroads $1.00 a barrel for shipping oil he could sell for only $2.50.

He and Hardison stretched their already tautly stretched credit even further. They shipped by sail 40 miles of 4-inch pipe around the Horn to Ventura and then built a pipeline to Newhall. In 1886 it was completed. Oil went by pipeline from the fields to Ventura, where it was put in barrels and shipped by water to San Francisco. Shipping costs were cut 50 percent. The total production for the partners in 1886 was much larger that year—35,350 barrels. But they were still in deep financial trouble. About the only thing that kept their families fed was the income from a few wells in which they still held an interest back in Pennsylvania.

And in Pennsylvania a curious man got off the train one day in August 1886 and began to ask questions of anyone who would talk to him about any facet of the oil business at all.

Although there were large numbers of immigrants with foreign accents working in the oil fields, Adrian Stoop learned that a foreigner seeking information about the oil business for a foreign firm was regarded with suspicion and even hostility. He stopped telling people that he was an employee of the Royal Dutch East Indies department of mining sent to Pennsylvania to learn about oil-well drilling.

Stoop was in the oil fields 100 days, and he spent every day, and most nights, hard at work. When he set out for home again, he had compiled information on everything connected with oil —the methods used to find it, to drill wells, to cap gushers, to transport it, to refine it, to package it, and how to make the packages (cans and barrels). He even translated and digested the laws passed controlling oil and oil producers.

When he got back to Sumatra, he found that while other wells drilled in his absence by crews under Zijlker had been either dry or disappointing, there was an interesting phenomenon at the second well they'd drilled. Telaga Toenggal No. 1 had come in at 5 barrels a day. It was now producing, for reasons unknown, 144 barrels a day. (That well was still producing about 200 barrels a day when the Japanese invaded Sumatra in 1942.) But that was the only bright light in the Sumatran fields. The money Zijlker had raised was now exhausted, and the government, which had been lending additional support, withdrew.

There was only one slim chance, and that was to go back to Holland to the same bankers and make the same arguments all over again. Zijlker boarded a ship for the long trip home and found himself sharing the captain's table in the dining saloon with N. P. van den Berg. Van den Berg was a banker, formerly head of the Bank of Java, and was on his way home to reap the good things of life sixteen years in far-off Java had earned him.

Zijlker decided that no harm would come of practicing his arguments on van den Berg, who was, after all, a banker and could be expected to react like one. He succeeded beyond what he thought possible. Not only was van den Berg impressed with the potential of an East Indian oil business, he was so enthusiastic he wanted to run it. He abandoned his thoughts of retirement, and by the time the ship docked in the Netherlands, the two had drawn up the necessary papers.

Zijlker, the last time he'd been in Holland, had gotten nothing from the bankers but polite (and sometimes impolite) suggestions that he was a dreamer or a schemer or a con-man or all three. Van den Berg didn't even go to the bankers until he'd made a call at the royal palace. He came out of the palace with the permission of King William III of the Netherlands to let it be known that the van den Berg-Zijlker operation had His Majesty's moral support.

A prospectus was issued for a company with an awesome title, Royal Dutch Company for the Working of Petroleum Wells in Netherlands India, Inc. (Naamlooze Vennootschap Koninlkijke Nederlandsche Maatchappij tot Exploitatie van Petroleumbronnen in Nederlandsch-Indië), and 1,100 shares at 1,000 guilders each were put on the market. The issue was oversubscribed 4½ times, and would-be investors were allowed to buy a fraction of the shares they wanted. The title of the company was too long even for native Hollanders to use with ease. They began to call the company "Royal Dutch."

Zijlker, who contributed far more to the development of the oil industry in Asia than Drake had in America (all Drake had done was drill the first well; Zijlker had found the oil, arranged for financing, and drilled the first well) was not to see the business develop. He dropped dead in Singapore less than six months after Royal Dutch was formed.

He and van den Berg, defying the tradition that company presidents had to be at least sixty years old, had picked as president of the new company a naval engineer half that age, J. A. de Gelder. De Gelder got together with Stoop and, using the data Stoop picked up in Pennsylvania, began to plan an oil industry from well to refinery without ever having seen either.

He proved himself an oil man who would have been at home in Pennsylvania or California, taking chances and spending money with an abandon that terrified his staid backers. He went to Belgium and ordered a tank farm and a railroad bridge to be fabricated in Europe like an erector set and shipped in pieces to Sumatra, where it would be reconstructed. He went to France and ordered the rails for the railroad he was going to build and the locomotives and tank and flat cars which would run on it. He went to Germany and ordered a take-apart agitator, and he ordered vast quantities of flat steel and tin from England's steel mills.

Only in the matter of actually drilling the wells did he show any doubt that anything the Americans could do, Royal Dutchmen could do better. He sent two young graduates of Holland's Delft University to Pennsylvania armed with open minds and open checkbooks. In Pittsburgh, to get their feet wet, they bought a refinery and saw it crated and started on its long trip to Sumatra. In New York City they bought a tin-can factory and a wooden-box factory and crated those up and sent them off to Sumatra. And then they asked around for the names of the best tool pushers and rig builders, which was their real reason for being in the United States. Shortly afterward, on the Royal Dutch payroll at more than they'd ever earned in the United States and traveling first class, W. B. Montgomery, driller; T. E. Bradish, tool dresser, rig builder, and stillman; D. Muir and H. Johnson, stillmen, sailed for Sumatra.* They were followed a year later by H. H. Beers, a petroleum specialist, J. Keefe, an-

---

* The rig in use was the cable type, where the hole was dug by the pounding of the tool bit into the earth. The driller (sometimes "tool pusher") was in charge. The tool dresser kept the bit sharpened, or "dressed." The stillmen (from distillery, refinery, or "still") built and operated the fractionating tower.

other stillman, and W. M. Montgomery, the other Montgomery's brother and, like him, a rig builder and driller.

They were the first of an army of American oil men to head for far-off places at enormous wages to work oil fields. It was sound decision on de Gelder's part. In the midst of the jungle, using native labor, an American-style oil field, complete from drilling rig through refinery to can-making machinery mushroomed and went on stream much sooner than de Gelder had thought possible.

The success was due as much to the willingness of a Dutchman named J. B. August Kessler (whom de Gelder had dispatched to Sumatra to run things in his name) to go along with the Americans as it was to American expertise in the oil business. His philosophy apparently was that since they were being paid so much to make Royal Dutch a success, they should be encouraged to do it their way, even if the way they were doing it rubbed staid Dutch colonialists the wrong way.

The only product of the first Royal Dutch refinery was kerosene. Sixteen hundred five-gallon cans (three hundred barrels) packed two to a wooden case came off the line every day. Kessler arranged for his product to be tested against American and Russian kerosene. Perhaps not surprisingly a kerosene refined by colonial Hollanders was judged by other colonial Hollanders to be superior in every way to the competition, and this judgment was proclaimed in the newspaper, *Penang Gazette*, which went on to state, on April 9, 1892, "that this oil, if matters are managed right, is in a position . . . to dominate the markets of the Far East."

Despite the glowing future predicted by the *Gazette*, Royal Dutch nearly went broke in its early days, partly because of a dip in the market (Standard Oil was selling kerosene in the Far East, too; its method of dealing with the competition there was to sell its product at a price lower than the competition's, without regard to production costs. Eventually, the idea went, the competition would go broke, whereupon Standard could charge whatever it wanted), and partially because even when fellow Dutchmen loyally bought the Dutch product, it was several months or longer before the cash returned to the refinery.

There was a young Dutchman named Hendrik W. A. Deterding in Sumatra, the subagent in charge of the Penang office of the Netherlands Trading Society. The NTS was the apparatus set up to handle the business affairs of the various Netherlands commercial enterprises in the Orient—shipping, banking, relations with the natives, and so on. It functioned very much like the British Hudson's Bay Company in Canada. When Royal Dutch was desperate for money, H. W. A. Deterding had the NTS bank loan one florin to Royal Dutch for each case of refined and canned kerosene put into storage in an NTS warehouse.

The loan saved Royal Dutch. It was a sound loan for Deterding's bank, a patriotic gesture on the part of a Dutchman toward other Dutchmen, and contained a certain element of enlightened self-interest for Deterding. De Gelder resigned in May 1892, and Kessler took his place. Deterding joined the company in July 1896 at age thirty. At age forty, in 1906, he became the general managing director of what had become the Shell Group Companies, a position (which, in European business circles combines the authority, responsibility, and pay of both president and chairman of the board) he held until 1936.

chapter 6

BY 1890 HARDISON AND STEWART MANAGED TO accumulate property, wells, refineries, and pipelines in California worth about $1,800,000. However, they were still in deep personal debt and living from day to day. They finally got together with a man named Thomas R. Bard, a wealthy landowner who had been dabbling in oil. On October 17, 1890, they incorporated as the Union Oil Company of California, with an authorized capital of $5,000,000.

It consisted of three producing companies (Hardison & Stewart; Sespe; and Torrey Canyon) and the Mission Transfer Company, in which Bard had originally owned the controlling interest. Bard was named president of the company, although Hardison and Stewart controlled 53 percent of the stock of Union Oil. The company started with 26 wells, which had in 1890 yielded about one-quarter of all California production, about 85,000 barrels.

There was almost immediately a clash of wills between Lyman Stewart and Thomas Bard. Like most businessmen who invested in oil at the time, Bard regarded it like coal or timber, a natural resource which should be gotten out of the ground and sold as quickly as possible to provide money to invest in other, more substantial projects. Stewart held an almost exactly opposing view of the oil business. He wanted to build an industry, which would take out of the ground only the oil required for its own refining and selling operations. Most importantly, rather than taking money out of the business to invest, for example, in the orange groves around the little town of Los Angeles, he wanted to put it right back into the company, primarily to acquire more producing land.

Internecine warfare began immediately. Bard was a multimillionaire with a large cash income. Hardison was better off financially than Stewart, who was at the bottom end of the financial ladder. One of the first acts of the Union Oil Company's board of directors was to vote President Bard, who didn't need the money, an annual salary of $5,000. Vice-President Stewart, who was actually worried about putting food on the family table was given a $5.00-a-day salary for his full-time services.

Bard had seen to it that an ally of his, I. H. Warring, was named secretary of Union Oil. Bard had many other business interests, and it was his intention to have Warring stand in for him at the company when he wasn't there. Warring delighted in snooping around and reporting what he found out to his mentor, Bard.

Lyman Stewart retaliated by waiting until he knew Bard was out of town, then convening a meeting of the company with himself as acting president and committing the company to large expenditures of money for land, production facilities, and pipelines. Warring would then run to Bard to report with righteous indignation what the vice-president had done. This was followed by an acrimonious meeting of the board of directors with Bard presiding. Lyman Stewart usually won. But the disagreements between Bard and Stewart soon reached a point from which there was no chance whatever of reconciliation because each regarded the other as a fool.

Bard wanted to take company profits and put them where they would do some good; Stewart held out for reinvesting two dollars of profits in land for every dollar paid out as dividends. Since he was barely keeping his head above water on his five dollars a day, this can only, on reflection, be considered a demonstration of corporate loyalty on his part. It would have been much easier for him to take the dividends and raise his own standard of living.

But Bard's position evokes some sympathy, too. He had millions of dollars tied up in Union Oil and as a practical business-man felt entitled to some return on his investment. His vice-president seemed determined to keep Union Oil on the edge of bankruptcy.

Hardison, meanwhile, seemed to be slipping over to Bard's side. He wanted to get out of the oil business and into something more respectable. He was still Stewart's close friend, but he an-

W. L. Hardison, cofounder of Union Oil Corporation.
Photo taken about 1890. UNION OIL PHOTO.

nounced that he would sell his stock to Stewart as soon as Stewart could afford to buy it. That left the large question hanging of what Hardison would do if Bard offered him a good price for his stock.

Stewart, absolutely convinced there was more in petroleum than kerosene, naptha, asphalt, and grease, was spending money on a laboratory at the refinery. Bard regarded this as absolutely frivolous—a shameless, perhaps even criminal waste of the company's money.

Then one day in 1891 there came a letter from Standard Oil, offering to contract for all of Union's naptha and gasoline production. This, Warring knew, was precisely the deal Bard wanted. If Union sold gasoline and naptha to Standard, it would do so in large quantities; and there would be a large check deposited to its account as soon as Standard took delivery. Warring ran to Bard and Bard trotted to the office to dictate an acceptance, only to find that Lyman Stewart had already turned Standard down flat, in another example of his portentous prose: "We cannot believe that it would be to our advantage to ask you to handle for us . . . our products . . . especially such as meet with so ready a sale at a satisfactory price. . . ."

There followed, of course, another meeting of the board. Vice-President Stewart was upheld over President Bard, which annoyed Bard more than a little. He encountered with some sonorous prose of his own, directed to Stewart's good friend, F. H. Dunham, who was the dignified, responsible director of the refinery. "It will be your duty," Bard wrote, "to keep the gates of the refinery under lock at all times. You will report once a week the names of the persons admitted to the yard. You are enjoined from imparting to anyone any information relating to the work of your own or any other department of the company's business, except as you may be permitted to do under special written instructions." The memo writing (there was a steady stream of them, all as insulting as this one) was calculated to enrage

Dunham so he would quit. Counseled by Lyman Stewart to ig-
nore both the memos and the company president, Dunham
stuck.

Then at a meeting of the board in July 1892, Bard won this
particular battle. The board was probably more than a little
annoyed with Stewart and decided to indulge Bard just once. It
was moved and seconded and carried that Dunham be dis-
charged. Then, just to show where their sympathies lay, it was
moved by one Bard board member, seconded by another, and
then carried that Vice-President Stewart be appointed a committee of one to tell Dunham that he had been fired.

Previously, for no reason other than enraging Stewart, Bard
had hired a chemist to replace Lyman Stewart's chemist. Dr.
Frederick Salathe, a Swiss, was hired at $10,000 a year. Then he
was put in charge of the Santa Paula refinery and given a free
hand. The first thing he did was to stop furnishing reports of how
much oil had been refined, which threw the sales organization
into utter chaos. Next he began to devote all of his time to a
special project of his own, the manufacture of sewing-machine
oil. He ultimately came up with a fine sewing-machine oil and
put the refinery to work making 300 barrels of his pride and joy.
Since sewing-machine oil was customarily sold in ½-ounce cans,
this was enough for 1,612,800 cans. There weren't that many
people in California, and there probably weren't that many sew-
ing machines in the entire United States, but Bard wouldn't hear
a word said against his protégé.

Stewart's land-buying policies were paying off. He managed
to control one meeting of the board which authorized the purchase of the Los Angeles Oil Company, which held 800 acres of
promising land in the Los Angeles basin. The purchase price
was more than Union had in the bank, but that didn't bother
Stewart at all. Bard stood by fuming as arrangements were made
to borrow still more money. His temper didn't cool a degree,
even after one well came in to produce 15,000 barrels a year

Union Oil derricks in the Adams field, Ventura County, California, 1892. UNION OIL PHOTO.

nor even after Adams No. 28 came in on February 28, 1892, gushing 1,500 barrels a day and making the loan unnecessary. Before that well, the biggest yet in California, could be capped, it had gushed out 40,000 barrels of oil, so much that it overflowed the tanks, the pumps, the hastily built dirt reservoirs and then flowed down the Santa Clara River and into the open sea. Once capped, it settled down to a steady 200 barrels a day (73,000 barrels a year).

Some of the battles between Stewart and Bard were ludicrous, and some were even sad; but either way they were costing the company money. Stewart, at great effort, had finally convinced Gen. M. H. Sherman (a bona fide former soldier, for once) who was president of the Los Angeles Consolidated Railway Company, to install oil burners in the railway shops. Stewart knew, because Sherman told him, that the only reason the railway was willing to try oil was to save money. They were having financial trouble, and economy was important. Furthermore, the railway would be a little late with the first couple of payments. Stewart was delighted. He knew that Sherman would learn he could heat his boilers and heat-treating furnaces and metal molding apparatus better and cheaper with oil than he could with coal. It would be a large and steady market for Union Oil, and a slight wait for the money was nothing to be worried about. The railway was solid.

So far as Bard was concerned, anything that Stewart was for, he was against. General Sherman, a proud man who considered his word his bond, received a short note from Bard telling him, "We shall certainly decline your orders unless we can be insured against inconvenience occasioned by dilatory payment." Sherman's response was predictable and immediate. He switched his oil purchase orders to a Union competitor who was delighted to wait a year or longer for payment.

Early in 1894 Lyman Stewart, who had been in California for ten years, decided it was time to return to Pennsylvania and have a look at his investments there. Before he left, he arranged for his son Will, then a student at the University of California, to learn something about oil refining by working as a laborer at the Santa Paula refinery. Young Stewart had already worked as a laborer on the rigs in the fields, learning that facet of the business from the bottom up.

When Stewart returned from the East, he found that Warring had issued orders barring Stewart from the refinery. Lyman Stewart took Will from the job Warring had assigned him (banging steel loops in place around wooden oil barrels) and put him back to work in the oil fields. Then he went looking for Bard, and there followed a heated exchange of views concerning Mr. Warring. No conclusion was reached.

A few weeks later, on July 24, 1894, Bard waited until both Lyman Stewart and William Hardison were out of town and called a meeting of the board of directors. He resigned as president of Union Oil and saw to it that a crony of his, D. T.

Perkins, was elected president and that Warring was named general manager of all Union Oil Corporation operations.

It took Lyman Stewart three months to answer that. In October 1894 there was another meeting of the board of directors. This time Stewart controlled the voting stock. D. T. Perkins was fired, and Lyman Stewart was named president and general manager of union.

Having flexed his muscle, he now tried conciliation. He offered the ousted Bard the right to name five of the nine members of the board of directors, providing Bard agreed to stop harassing him. Bard, with no other option, accepted. A deceptive peace began.

So far as Stewart was concerned, the major problem for Union at the moment was Standard Oil. Standard, as a result of certain questionable deals with the railroads and because of the quality of its Eastern crude oil, was able to market in California an Eastern kerosene of better quality than California kerosene and at a cheaper price.

Stewart's proposed solution to the problem was to hire Professor S. F. Peckham, a distinguished chemist on the faculty of the University of California, to work on both improving the quality of California kerosene and reducing the costs of refining it.

Dr. Salathe's contract was not renewed. Peckham took over the operation of the refinery as well as the laboratory, and Lyman Stewart quietly rehired F. H. Dunham, the former refinery manager whom Bard had forced him to fire.

With the refinery back in competent hands and with a first-rate chemist at work on the problem of quality, Stewart could now devote his time to both land and markets. Stewart was convinced that oil was a better fuel for locomotives, in terms of both efficiency and cost, than coal. Furthermore, it annoyed him greatly to have coal-burning engines hauling trains of oil tank cars.

After several initial failures Stewart's mechanics finally provided a Southern Pacific Railroad locomotive with an efficient burner and fuel feeding system. But instead of an order, Stewart got a bill for expenses from Southern Pacific and shortly afterward learned that the SP was buying its oil from Standard. Then both the SP and the Santa Fe went into the oil business themselves, drilling their own wells and laying their own pipelines to provide the fuel for their locomotives.

Stewart was having bad luck with oil as fuel for steamboats, too. He had talked the owners of the S.S. *Pasadena* into installing an oil tank on the deck, from which oil flowed by gravity to fire the boilers. The oil was heated into a vapor by steam, and at the dock the engine seemed to work perfectly. When the *Pasadena* put to sea, however, water got into the oil, and the fires went out. After it nearly capsized in heavy seas, coal-burning tugs had to tow the *Pasadena* ignominiously back to port.

Stewart calmed her angry owners by assuring them that there would be no water whatever in future oil shipments. Then he talked the owners of the tug *Waterwitch* into converting to oil. The *Waterwitch* promptly exploded. Undaunted, Stewart arranged for the ferryboat *Julia* (plying between Vallejo and Port Costa) to burn oil. The *Julia* blew up, killing several people.

The steamboat inspectors, reasonably, cancelled all permits for steam-powered vessels to burn oil. That meant the *Pasadena* had to be converted back to coal, and, more insultingly, Union Oil's first tanker, the *W. L. Hardison*, was forbidden to sail until she was burning coal. W. L. Hardison, who took understandable pride in the S.S. *W. L. Hardison*, called in all his favors in Congress and had the steamboat inspectors' ruling overruled.

Then the *Hardison* burned to the water line. There are two stories about why. The Union Oil Corporation history reports that a Chinese cook set her afire when a pan of his cooking oil burned. The Standard Oil of California history reports that one of the ship's officers tried to find out how much oil was in one of her tanks by lowering a kerosene lantern down into the hold.

However it happened, the Union Oil's pride and joy sat, a burned-out hulk, at the dock.

By the summer of 1895 Lyman Stewart was a tired and sick old man. On August 24, 1895, there was still another reorganization. Stewart resigned as general manager and saw to it that F. L. Richardson was hired for that post. He retained the presidency and arranged that the number of members of the board dropped from nine to five.

Each director was supposed to be chairman of a committee in his speciality. Lyman Stewart headed the field department committee, which meant that he was in charge of buying oil lands.

Lyman Stewart in 1895. UNION OIL PHOTO.

Bard was named chairman of the pipeline, storage, and transportation departments, which is where he wanted to use his influence. Ex-President D. T. Perkins was appointed to the board
to handle refinery operations, and Will Stewart was named to
the board and put in charge of the Los Angeles office.

Peace, both sides announced, would follow.

A month later, Richardson suddenly dropped dead, and Stewart had to take over as general manager again. In October there
was another battle. Stewart was unable to tolerate Warring any
more. At a board meeting more heated (if possible) than any
before, Stewart finally saw Warring fired.

The demand for Union products had been growing all the
time. In 1896 Stewart sent an entire shipload of asphalt around
the tip of South America to the East Coast. Railroads had converted to oil. There was demand for lubricating oils and greases,
naptha for cooking stoves, benzene for paint, and other distil-
lates used by city gas companies to enrich their coal gas. There
was even a growing demand for a product which previously had
been allowed to run away because it was useless: gasoline was
now used to power horseless carriages in ever-increasing quantities.

There was as far as Union was concerned, however, a black
side to the oil business, and it was spelled the Standard Oil trust.
The Standard Oil Company of Iowa was founded in 1885 when
Iowa Standard was merged with Continental Oil & Transporta-
tion Company. The Standard Oil trust, made up, among other
things, of sixteen other marketing companies like Iowa Stan-
dard, had carefully laid out areas of operation for each. Iowa
Standard's area of operations in 1885 was California and
Oregon. By 1900 its area also included the Hawaiian Islands,
Alaska, Idaho, Washington, Nevada, and Arizona.

Like the other components of the trust, it got its orders from
New York, where the offices of the Standard Oil trust were
located at 26 Broadway. The name "26 Broadway," at least in

the oil business, soon took on a life of its own. When people said "26 Broadway" they meant the Standard Oil trust, which was the same thing as saying "the Rockefeller interests" or even "John D. Rockefeller."

Rockefeller had taken a beating in 1892 in an antitrust suit before the Ohio Supreme Court and was maintaining a low profile, but there was little doubt that whoever held executive office within the Standard Oil trust did so with the approval of Rockefeller and could be expected to consult with him whenever necessary.

The control of 26 Broadway was exercised through the executive committee, and no officer in any operation of the trust could spend more than $5,000 for any plant investment without the approval of the executive committee. The executive committee also insisted on giving its permission before a pay raise could be given to any employee who made more than $50 a month. The fiction was maintained, however, that each of the companies making up the trust was a separate and independent operation.

When Standard of Iowa began to move into the California fields and market, it had five stations or depots—Los Angeles, Sacramento, Stockton, San Francisco, and Portland, Oregon. That year, it bought out Yates & Company in San Jose and built a station at Tacoma, Washington. In 1886 it opened stations in Seattle, Washington, and San Diego, California. In 1888 a station at Spokane, Washington, was opened. Between 1888 and 1893 stations were added at Marysville and Fresno, California, and in Vancouver, British Columbia.

Even before the mass movement to California in 1883, Standard was selling kerosene from horse-drawn tank wagons. By 1890 one-seventh of all Standard kerosene sales were handled by the wagons, and by 1900 one-third of them were. In 1886 the trust began to push lubricating oils and greases.

Its tactics were either (depending on who was making the judgment) a magnificent example of American enterprise at its best or a ruthless monopoly determined to push everybody else out of the market.

Col. E. H. Merrill was in charge of lubricating oil and grease sales. His boss back at 26 Broadway was Silas H. Paine. Paine began to write Merrill orders which were blunt and to the point: "Get Tubb's business at all hazards and regardless of cost," he wrote one time. Since it was necessary, according to the rules of 26 Broadway, to make a profit of at least 5 percent, Paine obligingly kept dropping the price of the lubricants to Merrill so that Merrill could undercut the competition and still make a paper profit of 5 percent.

Sometimes the iron fist in the glove showed through. In 1894, for example, the Standard agent in Portland, George C. Flanders, wrote a letter to a dealer in South Bend, Washington, who had the audacity to order a shipment of kerosene from the American Oil Company of Titusville, Pennsylvania. In the letter Flanders raged, "We do not propose to allow another carload [of American Oil's kerosene] to come into that territory unless it comes and is put on the market at one-half its actual cost."

John D. Archbold, who was to Rockefeller what Warring had been to Bard, was called before the federal government about Flanders's letter and passed it off casually as "a foolish statement, by a foolish man," but no one seemed upset about it, and, more importantly, no one fired or even disciplined Flanders.

There were other examples: A man named George W. Arper, a large wholesaler at Oakland, once dared to order some oil from the East. Standard agent Charlie Watson promptly paid a call on Arper to tell him, "If you bring oil in here, we will see that you don't sell it, and we'll drive you out of business."

In 1897 another wholesaler, H. S. Walker, had dropped a contract with Standard when it lapsed to make a new contract with two Eastern oil suppliers. He got a visit from E. S. Sullivan, the Standard agent in Los Angeles, who spelled it out clearly, "Walker, remember there have been others like you before. The

Standard takes good care of its friends. Those who are not its friends never remain in the oil business."*

In 1900 the threat to Walker was made good. Standard bought out the two firms (Arnold, Cheney & Company and the Penn Refining Company) from whom Walker had gotten his oil and then refused for two years to sell Walker any oil at all.

Independents defying Standard faced a number of threats. First was transportation, a major part of the price they had to pay for oil. Until 1887 it was perfectly legal for the railroads, in order to get a part of the vast Standard Oil shipping business, to pay Standard back a certain part of what Standard had been charged for transportation.

This became illegal with the passage of the Interstate Commerce Act of 1887, but it didn't really stop the practice. The second threat was Standard's willingness to go into a market and offer goods of equal quality for less than an independent could sell them for, frequently for less than Standard's cost of production, refining, and shipping. It preferred to lose money for a while—and could afford to lose money for a while—until the competitor went broke. Then it could charge whatever it wanted and recoup its losses. The final threat, to wholesalers who were buying their supplies in the East and who didn't buckle under to Standard, was simply to buy out the producer and refiner in the East. That left a wholesaler in the West with no source of supply.

* All the examples of high-handed Standard behavior given in this and the following chapter are from *Formative Years in the West,* a scholarly history of the Standard Oil Company of California by Professor Gerald T. White of San Francisco State College (New York: Meredith Publishing Company, 1962). The book was written with the full support of Standard Oil of California, who brought the book to my attention.

chapter 7

JUST ABOUT ALL OF THE RAILROADS WERE AS guilty as Standard Oil of offences which today would cause a long line of executives to march into the gates of a federal penitentiary. Oil from Pennsylvania fields traveling to the ever-expanding western markets could go one of two ways: by ship around the tip of South America, a four-month trip which cost about fifty cents per hundred pounds of petroleum product, or by rail, which meant by tank car.

The railroads announced that since they could find nothing liquid to ship back from California in the tank cars, it would be necessary to charge $105.00 in addition to the regular fee to get the tank car back to the East Coast. On the surface, this sounds a little stiff, but reasonable. It raised the cost of a gallon of kerosene about 2 cents.

Standard, however, wasn't bothered with this extra fee. It was using tank cars built under a patent issued in 1879 to a man named M. Campbell Brown. The Campbell Brown cars, to which Standard had acquired patent rights, consisted of a liquid tank at each end over the trucks and an open area between them in which it was possible to ship crated petroleum products as they would be shipped in a standard box car.

In theory, it was also possible to ship packaged goods from California back East in the cargo portion of the Campbell Brown cars. Although the cargo portion of the car was either soaked in kerosene or reeking of kerosene or both, theoretically this would not discourage shippers of foodstuffs or cloth or anything else, and the railroads announced they could not, in good conscience, charge Standard $105.00 to ship the empty car back. Standard Oil was thus given a 2 cents per gallon shipping advantage over its competition. And this isn't the only way in which the railroads were obliging.

In 1888–89 Standard shipped 9,178,000 gallons of kerosene to California. About a quarter of it went by sea, which took 4 months from the East Coast around the tip of South America to California ports. This meant that at any given time more than 2 million gallons of kerosene was just bobbing around on the ocean somewhere, not bringing any cash into Standard's coffers. It also meant that the railroads were losing one-quarter of the total business. It didn't take the railroads long to come up with a solution to the problem.

J. C. Stubbs, the general traffic manager of the Union Pacific, and E. A. Tilford of Standard had a meeting. The freight rate at the time was $1.25 per 100 pounds for petroleum products shipped from Cleveland to the West Coast. Under the new federal law, what the Union Pacific charged one customer was the rate it had to charge all customers. But the law didn't say how much the railroads had to charge, and it didn't forbid them from changing the price—that would have been unwarranted governmental interference.

Stubbs told Tilford (which is to say, UP told Standard) that if Standard let them know when its stocks in California needed replenishing, he would drop the rate per 100 to $.90. Standard would quickly contract for the shipment of as much oil as they needed at the $.90 figure. Then UP, having rented out all of its cars for, say, the next 60 days to Standard, would put the price back up to $1.25. This gave Standard another 2 cents a gallon profit and reduced the time-to-market of its products from 4 months to a couple of weeks.

At the same time Standard went to work on the clipper ship operators. Standard was still by far the largest shipper by water. To keep the clipper ship operators from lowering their prices to meet the railroad competition, Standard said it would not ship any oil at all by water unless the ship owners *raised* their prices (to everyone, of course, following the law to the letter) to $.60 per 100 pounds. This didn't give Standard any advantage in water shipment prices, but Standard made up for this when the oil reached the West Coast. Freight rates in California were high; it cost as much to ship oil from San Francisco to Bakersfield as it did to ship it from Pittsburgh to San Francisco. Until 1892 Standard was paying the Southern Pacific and Northern Pacific railroads (under one subterfuge or another) half what those railroads were charging everyone else.

Lyman Stewart's success (despite some setbacks) in developing a market for California-produced petroleum as a fuel struck the executive committee at 26 Broadway as a splendid thing. As early as 1891 they sent an oil scout of their own (J. L. McKinney of the South Penn Oil Company) out to California to look around. By 1895 they had decided to move into California production. Buying Union Oil itself seemed to be the best way to get into California as thoroughly and inexpensively as possible.

On July 13, 1896, Lyman Stewart was invited to San Francisco to meet with H. C. Breeden, the man in charge of Standard's San Francisco office. Breeden told him that he had been authorized by 26 Broadway to enter into negotiations to buy Union. Stewart, still broke, still worrying about meeting his monthly personal bills, seemed willing to sell with conditions. He told Breeden he would take $750,000 for one half of Union Oil (at $30 a share) or $1,300,000 for 65 percent of Union (at $40 a share.) He wrote his brother Milton a letter the next day in which he said, "If they deal, I will be out of debt. If not, I will just have to struggle along."

Although Breeden had announced that he had been authorized to negotiate, this wasn't the case. No officer of Standard was permitted to spend more than $5,000 of the trust's money without specific permission from 26 Broadway. On September 19, Breeden was told that 26 Broadway was not interested in Union Oil at those prices. There were some other negotiations, but it soon became apparent to Stewart that Standard wasn't really interested in buying Union. Since Standard was the only company with enough money to buy it, that meant he was stuck with it for better or worse.

Worse meant that he was still contending with Bard. In 1897 Union hired a civil engineer, R. W. Fenn. Fenn was a Bard man and served on the board of directors of Bard's Torrey Canyon Oil Company. But Fenn was an honest man, and Stewart admired him for that and for his knowledge of the oil business. Fenn was hired to do a survey of the entire Union Oil operation. Stewart probably figured that while Fenn was going to find things wrong with the way he'd been running the company, he wasn't going to find things wrong simply because Stewart had done them.

Fenn's report, by and large, supported Stewart. It stated that if Stewart had been permitted to build or buy the steamboat tankers he wanted that Bard had stopped him from acquiring, the company would have saved $600,000 in shipping costs. It went on to say that if they had had the pipeline Stewart wanted and Bard hadn't, which would have meant reduced costs, they could have kept the San Francisco market, which was now in the hands of Standard or Standard allies. Finally, after finding virtually nothing wrong with Lyman Stewart's operation of the company, it added that if Union Oil had followed Stewart's recommendation and purchased a tool and supply business to supply its own needs and to sell to others, this would have saved Union a "small fortune."

It was not what Bard expected to hear. He couldn't head off a board of director's decision to empower Stewart to build a 10,000 barrel tanker, but he again stopped the board from approving a pipeline or buying (or starting) a tool and supply business. Stewart got around the last veto by having Hardison & Stewart Oil start a tool business. Bard overrode him once the purchase had been made and insisted the business be sold.

While he was fighting Bard, a battle that seemed to grow more bitter by the day, Lyman Stewart had another deep concern—the morality of his workers. Throughout his lifetime, he never understood that men engaged in a rough-and-tumble business like oil were likely to speak pungently and to do a bit of drinking after a hard day's work. As the situation with Bard worsened, so had, in Stewart's opinion, oil-field morality. And that situation came to a head one sunny day in 1898 in the Torrey Canyon field.

Stewart, immaculate as always, walked gingerly through the muck to a rig. There were no child labor laws in those days, and boys from ten up held down whatever jobs they could handle. Stewart came across a very young boy, no more than twelve. The boy was working a hand bellows for a tool maker and was covered with sweat.

"Well, son," Stewart said to him, already planning to give the kid an easier job, "this is pretty heavy work for a fellow your size, isn't it?"

"Mister," said the innocent-faced lad, "she is a *** **** son of a *****, and you can tell the whole *** **** world I said so."

Stewart was horrified. He fled, for one of the few times in his life, and convened an emergency meeting of the board, at which the topic was oil-field morality. The only business conducted that day was authorizing the erection of a chapel in Torrey Canyon and the employment of the Reverend Mr. Johnson to tend to the souls of Union Oil workers in the fields.

While Stewart was plotting to save souls, Bard was plotting to take over Union. The details of what happened at the eighth annual meeting of the Union board of directors are quite confusing, but apparently Bard, quietly, had picked up support against Stewart on the Union board. With the votes he had as the man who controlled Torrey Canyon and some he could get from his share of Sespe Oil Company, he had enough to throw Lyman Stewart out.

Stewart learned of the plan on the day of the meeting. He was forced to the point of tears, but being a dignified gentleman, withdrew to an office so no one would see him. The meeting was held in the offices of the Torrey Canyon Oil Company, and the office in which Stewart sought privacy was Fenn's. Fenn happened to go into his office, saw Stewart's condition, and asked a few questions before making a startling announcement:

"Mr. Bard has forgotten that he has only two of the votes on the Torrey Canyon Board. That leaves you with a majority three."

"How do you figure three?"

"Your two and me," Fenn said, "I'll vote for you."

This time Bard's anger got the better of him. When the votes were counted, he went into a rage, accused Stewart of having bribed Fenn, and stormed out, threatening at the top of his lungs to "ruin the Union Company."

He tried to make good his threat. There were various complicated manuevers on Bard's part, countered by equally complicated manuevers on the part of Stewart (now with Fenn, who didn't take kindly to Bard's accusation that he'd been bribed, as a dedicated ally). Both sides formed new companies (Stewart, The United Petroleum Company; Bard, the United Stockholders Associates), neither of which had any purpose but to gain con-

A Union Oil California gusher. This is Lake View No. 1, first of the producing wells in that field. But Lyman Stewart, sure oil was to be found, had already built other drilling rigs.
UNION OIL PHOTO.

trol of Union Oil stock, so the other side could be thrown out.

Another in a long line of showdowns took place on November 28, 1899, at the annual meeting of the board of directors. The shares Bard owned or controlled were counted first. They came to 16,685. Then the shares that Lyman Stewart either owned or controlled were counted. He had 26,941. Bard was defeated, and Lyman Stewart lost no time rubbing it in. He had himself elected president, his son Will elected vice-president and general manager, and placed "Stewart men" in all the other executive positions.

Bard probably would have smarted more under his defeat than he did if he hadn't recently acquired a new job—junior senator from California. Furthermore, all he had lost was a little of the shine on his pride; his pocketbook was in great shape. But he didn't want to play second fiddle to Lyman Stewart, and it was now apparent that the last showdown was going to be just that: Stewart was not about to lose control of Union Oil again.

The word was passed that for the right price, Bard was willing to divest himself of his interest in Union Oil. Lyman Stewart made sure that word reached a young Los Angeles businessman, William R. Staats, a friend of his who he knew was looking for an investment. Bard's holdings were too much for Staats to attempt to buy himself, so he gathered around him some other young men with money to invest. Bard's holdings were still too expensive, so they were forced to turn to the banks for a loan.

One of the bankers to whom they turned, J. Henry Meyer of San Francisco, was faced with an interesting problem. He had a good deal of respect for Staats and probably even more for J. S. Torrance, one of the investors who had joined Staats in trying (with Frederick H. Rindge and John B. Miller) to buy Bard's holdings. But he also had a good deal of respect for Senator Bard's business acumen. If Union Oil was as good as Torrance, Staats, Rindge, and Miller thought, why was Bard willing to sell it?

He answered his own question by writing Bard and bluntly asking him. Bard's reply is interesting. "The Stewarts," he wrote, "are honest, and in the best sense, trustworthy. But they are not competent to carry on the great business of the company and are unwilling to trust it to more capable men." He said more, of course, but those two sentences probably sum up the differences between Stewart and Bard better than anything else that has been said.

Bard left Union Oil on December 18, 1900. Torrance, who replaced Bard as the spokesman for the minority, was easier to get along with than Bard had been, but he was no pushover. Years later, he explained his feelings about Stewart and Union Oil this way: "[I] regarded the service of Lyman Stewart as worth more to Union Oil than all the other directors put together . . . but I did not have very much respect for his ability as a financier."

Despite his opinion of Stewart's financial acumen, Torrance went along with Stewart's proposal to double the company's capital to $10,000,000. Torrance apparently liked Will Stewart, Union's general manager, and supported him in most of his decisions. Bard had often opposed young Stewart's moves simply because they had been made by Lyman Stewart's son.

One of Lyman Stewart's ideas about the training of Will Stewart in the oil business backfired. He made sure his son had learned the business from the ground up. Will had worked on the rigs, had worked in the refineries, had done every job any laborer or skilled workman on the Union payroll had done. He had learned the business, but he had not come to share his father's concern for the morality and behavior of the workers. As a matter of fact, Will Stewart was a welcome companion to drillers and tool pushers and mudmen and pipe layers in any oil-field saloon, where he could spit tobacco into a distant spittoon with the best of them and match any, when the occasion demanded, in the fine art of oil-field swearing.

The story of Lyman Stewart, Will Stewart, and the half-drunk drilling foreman quickly spread through the fields. Lyman Stewart went to his son and told him in a shocked tone that he had been at one of the rigs and learned that the foreman "came to work sober and then proceeded to become inebriated." It was clearly Will's duty to fire the man. "No man who starts work sober but ends up half drunk should be retained on the Union payroll," Lyman Stewart announced.

Will Stewart asked the man's name, and his father furnished it. "I know the man, Father," Will said, "and I can categorically state your information is incorrect. Not only does he not show up sober and then get drunk at work, but he is one of our best drilling foremen."

The Los Angeles field in 1895. More than 3,000 wells had been drilled on a narrow strip of land 4¼ miles wide. UNION OIL PHOTO.

Lyman Stewart took his son's recommendation and went away mollified. Will Stewart was then asked why he had given the foreman a good recommendation when it was common knowledge that sometimes he had to be carried home.

"He does not show up sober and then get drunk," Will replied. "He shows up drunk and gets drunker, but in the meantime, he's drilling some first-class holes."

At the other end of the oil business, selling what the drillers got out of the ground, Will Stewart began to have an influence. It was at his recommendation that Union Oil hired a salesman named John Baker, Jr. As soon as Baker went on the payroll, he started selling more oil than Union could produce. Will Stewart sent him to Hawaii. The largest consumers of energy in the Hawaiian Islands were the sugar plantations, who needed power to turn their sugar cane mills.

For years, there had been a neat arrangement providing coal for that energy need. Sailing ships carried Washington and Oregon lumber to Australia. They picked up coal from Australian mines and dropped it off in the Hawaiian Islands on the way home. Since they would have had to put worthless ballast in the holds anyway, they were able to turn a profit selling the coal for little more than they had paid for it.

After a couple of weeks in the Hawaiian Islands, Johnny Baker sold the plantation owners on the all-around superiority of oil as a fuel so well that Union couldn't deliver all the oil he sold. There followed a frantic period of activity which saw, before 1901 was over, 227,000 barrels of storage capacity built in Hawaii and the maiden voyage of the Barkentine *Fullerton* with a capacity of 16,000 barrels of oil, built simply to supply Hawaii.

Lyman Stewart was still borrowing money to buy more land than the Union treasury could afford. His wide reputation for piety, concern for lost souls, and being a Christian gentleman probably had more than a little to do with two loans (one for

$8,153 and the other for $16,400) he obtained in 1900 from the Los Angeles Diocese of the Protestant Episcopal Church.

Los Angeles had become the center of Union's operation. It was a rapidly growing city, and some of its more enthusiastic boosters were already predicting that one day it would stretch as far out in the country as Hollywood. In 1900 Union moved its head offices to Los Angeles, and when the Union Tool Company was organized on January 10, 1901 (it would not only work for Union, but make its services available to competitors), everyone agreed that it was a significant day in the history of the oil business. They were right. January 10, 1901, was a significant, historic day in the oil business, but not because Union had chosen that day to start its tool company. On the same day, on a little knob of land in the southeast corner of Texas, at half past ten in the morning, there was a rumble; then a thick gush of crude oil roared out of the ground and soared into the air over an oil rig put down by an ex-Austrian naval officer, "Captain" Anthony F. Lucas. Spindletop had gushed in, and another era beyond the imagination of those who preceded it had begun.

chapter 8

AS OF JANUARY 10, 1901, RUSSIA WAS THE LARGEST producer of oil in the world, with an annual production of 68 million barrels, or 186,000 barrels a day. California was producing 4 million barrels a year, and 53 million barrels were produced in the area called the eastern fields, which embraced Pennsylvania, West Virginia, Ohio, New York, and Indiana. Another 1 millon barrels came from Texas, mostly around Corsicana. There was also some small production in Wyoming, Kansas, Kentucky, and Colorado, all of it adding up to 58 million barrels in the entire United States. There was also some oil production in Rumania, in Austria-Hungary, and in the Dutch East Indies, and that was it.

Of the 58 million barrels produced in America, Standard Oil actually produced about 22 million barrels and bought 85 percent of the rest, at a price that averaged $1.13 a barrel. Since Standard was buying so much oil, what Standard was willing to pay for it set the price throughout the industry.

The history of Spindletop goes back to the 1880s and to a man named Pattillo Higgins. He was born in Beaumont, Texas, the son of the town's only gunsmith. After a series of escapades, during one of which he lost an arm, he left Beaumont (to the general relief of the respectable citizenry) and went up the Neches River to a job in a lumber camp. Stories drifted back to Beaumont that the loss of his arm hadn't proved much of a hindrance to him, either as a logger or as a saloon brawler. He was apparently as effective at settling a poker game argument with one hand as he had ever been with both.

When word reached Beaumont that Pattillo Higgins was on his way home, the reception planned for him was somewhat less enthusiastic than one planned for a conquering hero. He wasn't returning as a conquering hero, he said, but rather as something closer to the prodigal son. He had joined the Baptist church, he announced, and was henceforth putting the devil and all his wicked works behind him.

There was some skepticism about this complete turn-around, but as the months and then the years passed and Higgins not only showed up every Sunday at church, but stayed away from the saloons on Saturday night, he was gradually accepted as a sinner who had seen the light and used it to guide him on the straight and narrow path of righteousness.

He went into the real-estate business and eventually became a popular Sunday school teacher in the Baptist church. His exhortations to his students about the evils of cigarettes, whiskey, and wild women carried far more weight than similar exhortations from men who had never smoked, drunk, nor developed close relationships with saloon women.

Several miles outside Beaumont was a slight rise in the ground known as the Big Hill. Higgins used to take his Sunday school classes out to the Big Hill for picnics. There were several attractions. One was the Sour Wells resort, a collection of a half-dozen cypress boxes set in the ground holding "sour water." Some of the water was blue, some was yellow, some was green, and the rest was various shades in between. Some smelled like rotten eggs, some like lemon phosphate, and some like kerosene. The waters had certain medicinal qualities, too, some of it serving as an excellent laxative and others having quite the opposite effect.

Pattillo Higgins had also learned a peculiarity of the Big Hill. If the ground was soft (after a rain, for example) and a cane was stuck down into it for two feet or so and then withdrawn, gas would form in the hole and burn brightly for a while when ignited with a match. With proper magical incantations, this was a sure way to impress a Sunday school class.

But the most awesome phenomenon around the Big Hill was the frequent, if irregular appearance of Saint Elmo's lights. The hill would sometimes seem to glow with weird flashes of light, and there was no explanation for that at all.

Pattillo Higgins was becoming successful as a real-estate operator. He had quickly developed a skill for picking good farming land, or good land for business purposes. He invested the profits from his deals in land, and among the tracts he acquired was one of several hundred acres east of the Neches River in Orange County. That land was to put him in the oil business by the back door.

He came across an outcropping of clay on the land. He had it tested, and it turned out to be suitable for the manufacture of brick. At the time the bricks being used in that part of Texas came from the Northeast by ship down the Atlantic, around the tip of Florida, and then across the Gulf of Mexico.

There wasn't much demand for them, both because of the high cost and because most buildings were made of wood and no higher than two stories. Pattillo Higgins, however, was aware that some multistory buildings were already being erected ninety miles away in Houston and that more were planned.

Higgins went searching for capital to go into the brick business, using the simple argument that since he owned the clay and was only ninety miles from Houston (not two or three thousand as were the brick kilns of Massachusetts and New York), he could sell his bricks much more cheaply and still make a nice profit.

He quickly found financial backing and set off North to see how the brick business was run there. He went to Indiana, Ohio, New York, and Pennsylvania, and while he was compiling data on kiln size and temperature and other technical aspects of the business, he learned something else which fascinated him as much as the potential profits of the brick business. The kilns in the North were fired not by wood or coal, but by oil and gas, even when the kilns were located near or in coal fields. The petroleum fuels, he learned, not only were cheaper, but they permitted a temperature control not possible with any other fuel.

So, as an excursion from the brick yards, Higgins investigated the oil fields of Pennsylvania and New York. When the oil men told him how they found oil by looking for certain physical characteristics of the earth, it quickly became apparent to him that what the oil men were looking for in Pennsylvania he had on the gulf coast of Texas.

After he had the brick business going, he decided, he'd look into the oil business. But as soon as he got back to Texas, he found that the money he was supposed to get to start the brick business had been invested while he was gone in a furniture business.

Higgins's next step was to write the federal government for information on the location and production of oil. The government sent him a large and scholarly tome full of information, including the pronouncement that no oil-bearing rock and, thus, no oil could be found along the Texas gulf coast.

Higgins decided the government experts were dead wrong. He was not only sure there was oil around Beaumont, he was sure precisely where it was—on the Big Hill. There might not be enough of it to make him an oil millionaire or to make Standard Oil blink, but there was, he was sure, enough oil for local industry to use as a fuel.

When Pattillo Higgins had left town under a cloud to become a lumberman, the job had come from George Washington Carroll, president and general manager of the Beaumont Lumber Company. Carroll had wanted to help out his friend, Higgins's father. When Pattillo Higgins had returned from the wilderness, Carroll had been every bit as delighted as Higgins's father. He took a parental pride in knowing that he had been responsible in some way for bringing a sinner into the fold. When Higgins publicly renounced the devil, Carroll patted him on the back and told him that if he ever needed any help, he was available to give it.

Higgins went to Carroll, reminding Carroll of his offer and explaining his plans for the Big Hill. Carroll heard him out, loaned him a thousand dollars immediately, and put in a good word with several of his well-heeled friends and the bank. One of the friends was Capt. George Washington O'Brien, who had come by his rank honestly in the Confederate Army. Like George Washington Carroll, George Washington O'Brien was a pillar of the community. He had founded the Beaumont Methodist Church and was at the time grand master of the Beaumont Lodge of the Masonic order.

Carroll, O'Brien, and a third friend and pillar of the community, J. F. Lanier, got together with Higgins and formed the Gladys City Oil, Gas & Manufacturing Company. Gladys, whose photo adorned their stationery, was Gladys Bingham, an eight-year-old Sunday school student of Higgins's. The company went into business August 10, 1892.

Immediately things started to go, if not wrong, then somewhat less than smoothly. Higgins's three partners had reached their community and financial positions by careful, calculated, and cautious expenditure of their capital. Higgins's enthusiasm could best be described as hysterical. He wanted to drill for oil right then regardless of the expense. The partners, after passionate pleadings by Higgins, went along with little enthusiasm.

Over Higgins's objections the company hired M. B. Loomie, a Dallas sewage contractor to drill the well. Higgins was sure that

Loomie (and his subcontractor, W. B. Sharp) could not dig the well needed with the equipment they had. Loomie contracted to dig a 1,500-foot well in 6 months. When the time was up, he was down 300 feet. After a 2-months extension, he was down another 50 feet or so. He was fired, the money he had been paid was recovered from a performance bondsman, and another drilling contractor was hired. The second contractor did no better than the first; when his time was up he was still more than 1,000 feet shy of the 1,500 feet called for.

Meanwhile, Higgins had lost a good deal of respect in the community. He was subjected to ridicule, most of it along the lines of, "that was the sort of thing you could expect from someone like that." He was becoming an embarrassment to Carroll and O'Brien, who by now were willing to consider any proposition that would rescue them from the ridicule and give them a chance of getting some of their money back.

They told Higgins they would lease the property to him or anyone else he might be able to interest in taking it over. They would go even further than that: they would give him an option to buy the property and permit him to drill on the property during the period of the option providing, of course, that they didn't have to put up any more money and that their names wouldn't be connected publicly with the project.

Higgins confidently ran an advertisement in an Eastern business magazine, announcing that there was oil under Big Hill and millions to be made from it by someone "capable of adequately financing a proposition of some magnitude." There was only one answer to the ad. Capt. Anthony F. Lucas announced that he was on his way to Beaumont.

"Captain" Lucas was born in Dalmatia, then a portion of the Austro-Hungarian empire. He had studied mining at the University of Graz and then joined the Austrian navy as a midshipman. At the age of twenty-four, he managed to get himself commissioned into the Austrian navy as a lieutenant. But before going on active duty, he accepted an invitation to visit an uncle who had immigrated to Michigan. It didn't take Lucas long to compare the opportunities in America with those in Austria-Hungary, and he promptly resigned his commission and applied for American citizenship.

The first American custom he adopted for his own was that of self-appointment to high military rank. Before the ink was dry on his resignation, he had begun calling himself "Captain" Lucas and carefully pointed out that his rank was naval and the equivalent of the army's colonel.

Captain Lucas moved south, where in Macon, Georgia, he courted and married Caroline Fitzgerald, the daughter of a wealthy physician whose dowry permitted them to move to Washington, D.C., where he made himself available as a mining engineer. Lucas quickly found work locating salt deposits in Louisiana and then setting up mining equipment to exploit them. He wasn't a charlatan in this enterprise. Salt mining had been going on in Austria since before the time of the Romans, as the name of one of its most famous cities (Salzburg, or "salt castle") attests. He had been trained as a mining engineer, and he brought to the Louisiana salt deposits both knowledge and a capacity for hard work. He prospered and acquired a good reputation in a short time.

When Lucas saw Higgins's Big Hill, he shared Higgins's enthusiasm almost immediately. Lucas said that it was entirely possible they would find oil here duplicating the world's biggest well, which was 500 miles north of Baku in Russia and had produced 100,000 barrels of oil in 11 hours when it was discovered in 1893. Now, in the opinion of the people of Beaumont, there were two maniacs out at the Big Hill.

But Lucas backed up his judgment with cold cash. He took an option to purchase on 663 acres of land around Big Hill, putting up $11,050 in cash and signing notes at 7 percent for the balance to be paid in 2 equal annual payments. Higgins was given a 10 percent interest in Lucas's operation as a finder's fee, and George Washington Carroll, greatly relieved to have somebody else's money in the deal, said that he would add that much, paying Higgins from his profits, if any, from the deal.

Lucas put down a well, and while he found oil, it wasn't enough oil to pay expenses, much less a profit. And now Lucas found himself desperately trying to raise money. He could raise none in Beaumont; they knew too much about Higgins to pour good money after bad.

Lucas's reputation was such that he could get to see Henry C. Folger, a Standard Oil executive in New York who sometimes would advance money for an oil proposition, especially when a small loan would produce large potential profits for Standard Oil. Passing through Washington on his way to New York, Lucas stopped off to see Congressman Sibley of Pennsylvania, who was an oil man himself when not tending to the nation's business. Sibley laughed at him.

The next day in New York, Folger did not laugh. He was so impressed that he dispatched Standard Oil's expert in such matters, Calvin Payne, all the way to Beaumont from Pennsylvania to look over Lucas's property. On the way to Beaumont, Payne picked up J. S. Cullinan, a "former" Standard Oil executive who was now operating "independently" in Standard's Texas field at Corsicana.

These two experts examined Big Hill, and then Payne gave Lucas the summation of their judgment: "Captain Lucas," Payne said, "I have traveled around the world looking at oil fields in Russia, Rumania, Sumatra, and Borneo, and I have seen most, if not all, of the oil fields in the United States. The indications you have pointed out, while noteworthy and most interesting, have no analogy to any field I have ever seen produce oil. I do not believe there is any chance for oil here in paying quantities." Lucas protested and showed him a sample of the oil his first well had produced.

"Why don't you leave this risky and tricky business of oil to such people as Mr. Cullinan and myself," Payne said. "You have completely misled yourself here. You will never find oil here."

Payne, Lucas reminded himself, was probably the highest paid and, therefore, probably the best oil-field examiner in the business. Lucas had gone to great lengths to explain to him Higgins's rough theory and his own version of it.

It was revolutionary. The oil that had been found so far, according to Lucas, had been between the surface of the earth and the first thick layer of rock. The oil under Big Hill was under the layer of rock, some 1,000–1,200 feet below the surface of the earth. The oil that had bubbled up to make the "sour waters" had done so under pressure intense enough to force it through the rock strata.

So far as Payne, the recognized expert, was concerned, this was utter rubbish, not even worthy of a detailed rebuttal. Payne and Cullinan left Beaumont, and Lucas's morale sagged badly. It sagged even lower three weeks later when Dr. C. Willard Hayes of the United States Geological Survey, another highly respected expert, visited Big Hill and said the same things Payne had said.

Then came a very faint ray of hope. Dr. William Battle Phillips, professor of field geology at the University of Texas had a look at the Big Hill, said there might be something to Lucas's "nascent dome" theory of oil being under a rock strata, and gave him a letter of introduction to Guffey & Galey of Pittsburgh, Pennsylvania.

Guffey & Galey, using Mellon money, were at the top of their profession, which was finding oil where everybody said there was none. Andrew Mellon and his associates, who looked jealously at the money rolling into Rockefeller pockets from Standard Oil, were willing and able to make substantial investments in the hope of getting some oil money for themselves.

Guffey & Galey didn't bubble over with enthusiasm, but neither did they scoff. After some thought, they made an offer to form a partnership, Guffey, Galey & Lucas, with Lucas getting a very junior share. They would advance the money (which they would have to borrow from the Mellon interests) and they would see that one well got drilled. If the first well showed anything promising, they might drill one or two more, that decision being reserved to themselves.

What Lucas would have to do as his part of the bargain was first to maintain absolute secrecy, even with Pattillo Higgins. If there was to be a profit to Higgins, it would come out of Lucas's share, not the partnerships. And Lucas would have to get options on much more land than he presently held.

In May 1900 Lucas set about (with Guffey & Galey's money) leasing more land. He took over a 50-acre piece called the Chaison tract and the 5,300-acre Hebert tract on the south of the hill. He leased another 3,800 acres on the southwest of the hill. In all, including the original 2,500 acres of the Gladys City Company, he had about 15,000 acres.

The Big Hill itself, meanwhile, had been attracting other attention. Real-estate developers decided that in the future, people might want to buy lots there so they could take advantage of the breezes. The top of the Big Hill had to have a name with more sales zing, and after some thought the real-estate developers came up with one—Spindletop Heights.

Lucas couldn't buy all of this land, and one of the largest Spindletop Heights tracts, 33 acres about 100 feet from where he planned to drill the well, was a moral and ethical problem for him: Pattillo Higgins owned it. Lucas was sworn to secrecy about the Guffey & Galey deal, and if he tried to buy the tract for Guffey & Galey, Higgins was certainly going to ask questions of Lucas, who was his partner, too. Lucas resolved this by leaving Higgins's tract out of his acquisitions.

Lucas was having personal problems, too. There were so

many promoters around whose major interest in what they were promoting was to draw a salary from the company, that he told Guffey & Galey (as proof of his good faith) that he wouldn't take a salary. This had convinced Guffey & Galey of his good faith, but it also made it necessary for him to sell his furniture to feed his family. Lucas had come to Texas with a large bank account and a reputation both as a first class mining engineer and as a practical businessman. It was all gone.

John Galey hired two brothers, Al and Jim Hamill, to drill the well. Al showed up in Beaumont first to buy the lumber he would need to build the derrick and to establish a supply of wood to fuel the steam boiler which would power the drilling machinery. Lucas took him to George Washington Carroll, who was still president of the Beaumont Lumber Company.

Carroll made what seemed at first glance to be a generous offer. "Mr. Hamill," he said, "if you bring in a well that flows 5,000 barrels of oil a day, I'll make you a present of the lumber." Then Hamill and Lucas remembered that at the Corsicana field (the only field in Texas) a well that produced 50 barrels a day was considered first class.

Al Hamill asked Lucas where the railroad car full of pipe for the well was located. Lucas told him that the car had arrived in Beaumont and that he had been in touch with a house mover, who was preparing an estimate of what it would cost to unload the pipe and move it to the well site.

Hamill asked Lucas to show him the railroad car, and Lucas took him to it. Hamill took off his coat, climbed onto the car, and in a moment, a length of six-inch pipe came over the side.

"I'll roll it off," Hamill said. "You stack it."

In an hour the pipe (500 feet of 10-inch, 900 feet of 6-inch, and 1,200 feet of 4-inch) was stacked by the side of the rails. When the house mover appeared several days later with his estimate, he was told that his services would not be required.

Hamill had never built a derrick before, but by October 26

the derrick was up, and on October 27 the tool bit into the earth in the Spindletop subdivision for the first time.

The hole reached 60 feet, then 160 feet, and in 2 weeks was at 285 feet. Finally, they got a section of the smallest (4-inch) pipe down to 880 feet, where they encountered rock. They also encountered a small amount of oil, not enough to make a good (50 barrel-a-day) well, but oil. Then the pipe clogged, 300 feet of it filling with soft sand which the pumps couldn't handle. The 4-inch pipe string was pulled, and the 6-inch pipe was put down into the hole.

The larger pipe permitted drilling to resume, but they were now drilling into solid rock, which, so far as anyone knew, might extend miles into the core of the earth. The *Beaumont Journal* said that the major problem Lucas now faced was recovering the pipe in the hole, which was worth $4,000 and appeared to be all anyone could salvage from the operation.

Drilling operations closed down for the Christmas holidays of 1900 and didn't resume until New Year's Day, 1901. There was gas now coming out of the hole, posing problems both of asphyxiation of the crew and of explosion. The bit was now 950-odd feet down into the earth, slowing chewing solid rock into small bits which were then flushed to the surface with muddy water.

On January 2 there were rumors of fire at the well head, but Lucas explained that it was only the same Saint Elmo's fire that had been seen on the Big Hill for years. On January 9 the bit was at 1,020 feet, the last 140 of it through solid rock. It was now almost impossible to turn the bit. The force required snapped the chains providing power from the steam boiler.

Hamill announced that he had contracted to go to 1,200 feet with the well, and he would go to 1,200 feet if he snapped every link of chain in Texas. That same night, Lucas and his wife sat on the porch of their house, from which Spindletop was visible. There was more Saint Elmo's fire, and it seemed to settle right on the derrick.

At half-past ten in the morning of January 10, 1901, Lucas No. 1 came in in the Spindletop field, flowing 100,000 barrels per day. GULF OIL PHOTO.

"Doesn't Saint Elmo's fire have some meaning for seamen?" Mrs. Lucas asked, referring to her husband's nautical experience.

"The story is that when seamen see Saint Elmo's fire," Lucas told her, "it means their ship will come safely into harbor."

There was a spectacular display of the phenomenon that night, larger and longer than people could ever remember. And it turned out to be the last time Saint Elmo's fire ever appeared over Spindletop.

On January 10 with the first light the crew at the rig had pulled the string of pipe from the hole, one twenty-foot section at a time, unfastening each as the winch pulled it up. The sections were stacked against the derrick one by one until the bottom one appeared. The battered drilling bit, blunted and chipped by the rock through which it had drilled, was unfastened and a new one put in place.

One by one, twenty feet at a time, the pipe string was lowered back into the hole. Thirty-five sections, about seven hundred feet, were now hanging from the derrick, and another length was manhandled in place to be attached to the string.

Suddenly, down at the base of the derrick on the rotary table (which grasped the pipe and twisted it), mud began to spit out of the hole. No one thought much of it, because sometimes mud would splash that way when a pipe string was being replaced.

But instead of dying down, the flow of mud increased and then turned into a spout of mud. The crew decided that it was time to watch what was happening from a safe distance. They started to walk away from the derrick and then to run.

They ran just in time. The mud was now spouting as high as the derrick itself. And then something frightening began to happen. The pipe string came flying out of the hole, soaring into the air 100 feet, 150 feet, and the snapping off into what looked like pieces of spaghetti. It came to earth and stuck in the ground at odd angles. Then everything was quiet. The men shrugged. It would be a long, dirty, miserable job to collect all those pieces of pipe string from where they had scattered over the landscape, to straighten them, and to start drilling the hole all over again.

A short distance away Mrs. Lucas heard a noise like a cannon. She went out to the porch where she and her husband had watched the Saint Elmo's fire the night before. Then she ran into the house and telephoned her husband.

"Hurry, Anthony," she said, "something awful has happened. The well is spouting."

And spouting it was. Oil industry books report it with understatement. All they say is that at half-past ten in the morning of January 10, 1901, a well came in at 1,160 feet in what was to be known as the Spindletop field, flowing 100,000 barrels a day.

chapter 9

THE WELL WAS SHOOTING GREEN CRUDE OIL IN A stream six inches thick more than one hundred feet in the air. Almost the only man in Beaumont who didn't immediately become hysterical and stay that way was Captain Lucas. After his wife telephoned him that something awful was happening, he leaped into his buggy and raced to the well. He tasted the oil, saw what had happened, and then seemed to gain control of himself.

When a reporter for the *Beaumont Journal* asked him how much oil the well was flowing, Lucas told him 6,000 barrels a day. That was 1,000 over the 5,000 barrels he needed to get George Washington Carroll to pay for the derrick building materials, and 6,000 barrels a day made it by far the largest well ever found in Texas.

The gusher posed a problem. Oil spouting 100–150 feet into the air and then falling to the ground like rain can't be sold any easier than oil 1,200 feet below the surface. Lucas expected the gusher to die off. The largest well ever found before in the Baku fields of Russia had spouted for only 11 hours before stopping. Thereafter it was necessary to pump it out of the earth.

Spindletop showed no signs of slowing down at all, and as the days passed shutting it off became just as important as starting it up had been. When a carelessly discarded cigar butt set fire to a pool of oil from the well and almost reached the spout of oil itself, it became an emergency. Unless they could stop the gusher, all they were going to have for their effort was the world's largest torch.

The Hamill brothers set out to do what nobody had ever done before, to "cap" an oil well. The derrick itself and the work area around the hole were flowing in oil, some of it spraying out of the hole at angles as it left the earth and some falling back onto the rig after it spouted into the air. The first thing they had to do was get a relatively oil-free work area. Then they would have to come up with some means of corking the hole, through which oil was roaring at sixty-eight barrels (nearly three thousand gallons) a minute. What they came up with overnight was ingenious.

Basically, it made use of a T-shaped piece of pipe eight inches in diameter. The T would be put in place on its side, that is, with the two-ended piece placed vertically and the one-ended piece horizontally. Where the horizontal piece connected to the vertical piece was a valve, so that the flow could be directed into either the horizontal or the vertical piece of pipe. There were valves on the open ends of the horizontal and vertical pieces.

The T-shaped piece of pipe (the tee) was welded to a flat sheet of steel with a hole in it for the lower vertical section of the pipe, which was much shorter than the upper vertical section. The flat piece of steel, in turn, was attached to pieces of railroad tie, which were attached to the derrick itself.

The first thing the Hamill brothers did was to pull the pipe and plate arrangement over the gusher. The oil now gushed through the vertical pipe straight up. Then the valve was opened, directing the flow of oil out the leg of the tee, so that it wouldn't gush into the air and then fall back on the rig like rain.

There was still oil splashing everywhere, of course, so much oil (and so much noise) that the Hamill brothers and their crew had to wrap their faces in gauze and tape their ears shut with wads of cotton.

Once most of the oil was directed away from the rig, they forced the steel plate and the open end of the pipe downward onto the gusher with a block and tackle. The farther down they were able to force it, the more oil went into the pipe. Finally, they had the plate sitting right on the top of the hole. It was screwed into place with huge bolts, and the Hamills started to pack the joint to stop the high-pressure leaks. They used pieces of rope and wrought-iron clamps.

Finally there was no leakage at all, just the roar of three thousand gallons of oil per minute spitting out of the eight-inch pipe. Then the valves at the end of the pipes were slowly closed. The roar began to change pitch, to sound more shrill, but less and less oil was coming out of the pipe with each cautious quarter-turn of the valve handle.

And finally the roar died completely as the valve was closed. The Hamills and their crew again ran for safety; they had no idea whether the valves or the pipe itself or the steel plate was going to be strong enough to withstand the pressure.

It did, and finally there was a nervous laugh, "Why that silly looking pipe thing, looks like a Christmas tree, really works!" It was the first oil-field "Christmas tree," the name that is used today for what is more formally called a "well head valve assembly."

When word of what happened at Lucas Well No. 1 in the Spindletop field reached Pittsburgh, Pennsylvania, and the Mellon brothers, they didn't know what to think. They had grown rich and were to grow far richer by planning their actions clearly before they actually did anything, so that they were seldom surprised.

They didn't expect that Guffey & Galey were going to bring in the world's largest well. Their expert judgment of Guffey was that he knew enough about what he was going to do that he would be able to repay the $300,000 he had borrowed with interest.

When Spindletop came in, the Mellons were in business as T. Mellon & Sons, merchant bankers. The brothers were Andrew W. Mellon, who was later to become secretary of the treasury, and Richard B. Mellon. T. Mellon & Sons was to evolve into the Mellon National Bank & Trust Company.

They already had been in the oil business, moreover, and hadn't really liked it. In 1889 a nephew, William Larimer Mellon, actually had his bags packed to leave Pittsburgh to take over operation of a family-owned gas works. "Young Bill" Mellon was then twenty and not too pleased at the prospect of sitting in a gas-works office all day. Word reached him of a well that had come in on the outskirts of Economy, Pennsylvania, and he took off for the well rather than the gas works.

He liked what he saw, and he fortunately had two doting uncles with practically unlimited funds with which to indulge him. When he wanted to borrow a little money to go into the oil business, Uncle Andy and Uncle Dick broke out a stack of cashier's checks.

He either would make some money in the oil business, which, of course, would be all right, or he would go broke, in which case he would report to the family gas works a chastened young man, and that was all right, too.

Young Bill found oil, and he found it in such quantities that it made money for the family. A partnership was formed of the two uncles and the nephew, and Young Bill found more oil. This posed another problem. Standard Oil, which controlled the price of oil (it was buying about 90 percent of all the oil produced) was paying $1.13 a barrel for it. Young Bill reported that if they didn't sell their oil to Standard, they could probably get much more than $1.13 a barrel for it by selling it themselves along the Eastern seaboard. This wasn't enough for the Mellons to go into business in competition with Standard, but when Young Bill made a deal in New York to sell vast quantities of oil to a French concern at a price lower than what Standard Oil would charge the Frenchmen but substantially higher than what Standard would pay him for the same oil, the Mellons went into the oil business.

This was against the rules of the game: nobody could fight Standard Oil. The other side of that coin was that it was equally heretical to tell T. Mellon & Sons what they could or could not do.

T. Mellon & Sons went to the president of the Reading Railroad and got him to sign a contract to haul their oil from Young Bill's well to the Atlantic Ocean. T. Mellon & Sons had loaned both the Reading Railroad and its president money, and he didn't have much choice in the matter.

Standard Oil, on the other hand, regarded the contract as outrageous, disloyal, and absolute proof that the president of the railroad had lost his senses. At the next meeting of the board of directors, the president was fired, a new president installed, and T. Mellon & Sons informed that the Reading had no intention of honoring the contract the ex-president had signed. If T. Mellon & Sons wanted to sell their oil to Standard at $1.13 a barrel like everybody else, Standard would buy it. Otherwise, what they would have was tanks of oil in western Pennsylvania that no railroad would haul for them.

The ex-president of the Reading Railroad became an employee of T. Mellon & Sons. T. Mellon & Sons went to eastern Pennsylvania, bought a tract of land along the Delaware twenty miles south of Philadelphia at Marcus Hook, and started building a waterfront storage facility. T. Mellon & Sons then announced that hauling oil on the railroad was an inefficient means of moving it and that the best and most obvious way to move it was through a pipeline. They announced they were going to build a pipeline from their oil wells to Marcus Hook.

It wasn't the first time that Standard Oil had heard threats of this kind. They had had long experience in suppressing rebellion. But they had never come up against the Mellon brothers before. When Standard politicians in the Pennsylvania legislature introduced legislation in the public interest which coincidentally would have prohibited the Mellons from building their pipeline, they found themselves outvoted by Mellon politicians who introduced legislation in the public interest which permitted the Mellons to build their pipeline. When gangs of vandals, acting out of pure meanness with no connection whatever with Standard Oil, showed up to punch holes in the pipeline, gangs of hoodlums, acting out of pure public spiritedness with no connection whatever with the Mellon brothers drove them away. In November 1892 Young Bill Mellon stood atop a storage tank at Marcus Hook and watched as the first Mellon oil flowed through the Mellon pipeline from the Mellon oil fields 271 miles away.

There was only one course of action left open to Standard Oil, and the company took it. Out came the check book. The Mellon partnership sold out its wells, its pipeline, and the Marcus Hook facility to Standard Oil. The partnership made $2,500,000 in clear profit.

Young Bill, freed forever from sitting in a gas-works office, turned his attention to a new way to grow richer, the street railroad transit (or streetcar) business. Among themselves, the Mellons decided that while they had made an honest dollar or two, they didn't like the oil business. It wasn't the sort of thing gentlemen bankers did.

T. Mellon & Sons would, of course, continue as bankers to make good loans, including loans to people in the oil business, but that kept them in banking and out of oil.

It was under these circumstances that they loaned Guffey & Galey $300,000 to lease land and drill a well, much as they would have loaned someone with the same reputation that much money to go into the cattle business or the streetcar business, or any other business enterprise. They expected to get their money back with interest, which was the way you made money as a banker.

The Mellons had suggested to Guffey how the J. M. Guffey Company should be set up. Guffey got five-eighths of the company, Galey two-eighths, and Capt. Anthony Lucas, one-eighth. It was a carefully thought out, logical, businesslike way to loan money and get it back with interest.

And then Spindletop, or Lucas No. 1, came in.

As soon as Lucas No. 1 had been capped, Guffey & Galey started another hole and then a third. Patillo Higgins was now able to get all the money he needed to drill a well, and a derrick quickly went up on the strip of land he owned outright on Spindletop Heights. A driller named D. R. Beatty was the first man to bring in the second well.

Beatty had been in Galveston on January 10 when he got word of the gusher. He was aboard the first special train to Beaumont, having left in such a hurry that he had only twenty dollars in his pockets. He made his first deal with a poor farmer, Lige Adams, who owned a small farm half a mile from Lucas No. 1. Adams gave Beatty a lease with two important considerations. The first was that drilling start within thirty days, and the second was that he be hired as cook to feed the drilling crew. He needed a cook's wages (in which he could believe) just about as much as a royalty on oil (in which he could not believe).

It took Beatty about a month to get a rig built on the Adams property and another month to drill the hole. On March 26, 1901, it came in, and it was a gusher. Shortly afterward, the second and third holes Guffey & Galey had put down came in, and so did the first hole Pattillo Higgins drilled on his own. Every one was a gusher.

Everybody seemed to be getting rich around Spindletop. A clerk in a grocery store managed to scrape together $60 with which he bought 4 acres of land. Shortly after Lucas No. 2 and

Lucas No. 3 came in, he was paid $100,000, cash, for his land. There were other stories, repetitions of the theme that what had been, before Lucas, rather poor farming land was, after Lucas, valuable beyond most people's comprehension.

By May 1901 the Mellon brothers had decided it was time they went back into the oil business. The J. M. Guffey Petroleum Company was formed with a capitalization of $15 million. R. B. and A. W. Mellon (the uncles) bought 10,000 shares each at $30 a share. They sold to 6 of their friends another 30,000 shares. In other words, for $1.5 million the investors bought one-third of the new company. The money went to Guffey in exchange for the J. M. Guffey Company. He was also given 70,000 shares of the new company.

From the $1.5 million Guffey was supposed to buy out Galey and Lucas. Lucas, aware of what he had, bargained hard. For his one-eighth interest in the original company, he accepted $400,000 and 1,000 shares of the new company. Galey came cheaper. He sold his two-eighths interest for $366,000 and some other oil stocks Guffey owned and Galey wanted.

Five months after Lucas No. 1 came in, Guffey was majority owner and president of an oil company which he valued at $18 million. The company owned 4 producing wells at Spindletop, and 4 more were being drilled. There was a 6-inch, 16-mile pipeline from Spindletop to Port Arthur, a million-barrel storage facility (65,000 barrels at the field, the rest at Port Arthur), a million acres of leased land in Texas and Louisiana, 375 acres of land owned outright (most of it at Port Arthur), and some other assets.

But the assets weren't quite enough to make money with the new company. There were no refineries, no tugs, barges, or ships to move the oil, and the 100 railroad tank cars the company owned had no more than 16,000-barrel capacity, about what one of the 4 wells was producing in half a day.

The 30,000 shares of stock held in the company treasury were put on the market at the best possible time. Andrew Carnegie, a Scottish immigrant who had founded the Carnegie Steel Company, had been rewarding his employees with stock in his company. When J. P. Morgan bought him out (to found the U.S. Steel Company with Carnegie property as the nucleus) the employees were paid in cash for their shares of Carnegie stock.

One bookkeeper, for example, who had been earning $32.50 for a 48-hour week was handed a check for $1,900,000 for his share of the company. He and the others then looked for places to put their money to work. The Mellons had a good reputation, and when the Guffey Petroleum Company stock was put on the market at $30, competition to buy it soon drove the price to $66 a share. By May 1902 the stock was worth $95 a share.

Guffey was getting rich in Texas, but he only visited Spindletop, the source of the vast bulk of his fortune, once. He was

The forest of drilling rigs at Spindletop in 1902.
GULF OIL PHOTO.

asked about this years later and was quoted as saying, "Northern people were not very well received in Texas, then."

The Mellons had suggested, and Guffey had agreed, that for business reasons a separate company should be set up to refine and sell the oil produced by the Guffey Petroleum Company. In June 1901 Guffey wrote his general manager, J. C. McDowell, telling him that the executive committee (which, in practice, was the Mellon brothers and Guffey) had proposed that the refining and marketing company be called the Texas Oil Refining Company.

McDowell wrote back that there already was a company using a very similar name and that it had been formed just a few weeks before by a group of men who would probably be unwilling to give the name up, even for a price. The original Texas Company, which grew into Texaco, had been founded by J. S. Cullinan, J. W. Swayne, and former Governor James M. Hogg. Most of the capital had come from a flamboyant ∤ntrepreneur of the oil fields, John W. Gates. Always willing to bet any amount of money on a business deal or a poker hand, he was known as "Bet-a-Million" Gates.

Guffey and the Mellons wanted a name suggesting where the company got its oil. Since Texas was not available, they looked to the next geographic feature, and the Gulf Refining Company of Texas was formed. It's interesting to speculate that if there had been a couple of weeks difference in forming the two companies, Gulf might now be Texaco, and Texaco, Gulf.

Gulf Refining was legally a separate company, but Guffey was president of Gulf as well as of Guffey, and Guffey again was the majority stockholder, with 41,673 of the 150,000 outstanding shares. The Mellon brothers took 16,483 shares each. There were other stockholders, including Charles M. Schwab, the founder of Bethelehem Steel, who owned 5,000 shares, and James Galey, who owned 2,000.

Legal battles started almost as soon as Lucas No. 1 came in.

On May 1, 1901, just when the Mellons and Guffey were forming their company, Pattillo Higgins filed suit against both Lucas
and George Washington Carroll. The suit against Lucas demanded payment of the 10 percent interest Higgins felt he had
in the well; he asked for $4 million. The suit against Carroll
demanded that Carroll pay him $200,000, 10 percent of the $2
million Carroll was supposed to have made as his share of the
profits. Both suits were settled out of court. Carroll and Higgins
remained close friends, but while there was no public demonstration of ill-will, Higgins never entered into another business
deal with Lucas.

The multimillion dollar figures in the suits, however, set off a
fire of their own. The oil boom made the gold rush seem tame.
Every train coming into Beaumont was loaded with people determined to get their share of the oil millions even though they
knew nothing whatever of the oil business. Six trains a day were
scheduled into Beaumont from Houston, and there were special
trains whenever the railroad could fill up the cars and find a
locomotive.

Before Lucas, the Crosby House had been Beaumont's best
hotel in a time when that term meant, by and large, ladies ex-
changing polite gossip in a hushed lobby while their men, in
voices just as politely muted, exchanged their gossip in the men's
salon. Immediately after Lucas, the men's salon became the
men's saloon, with customers packed six and eight deep shouting
for drinks around the clock. The lobby took care of the over-
flow, and while there were still women in the lobby, they could
not, even by stretching the term, be called ladies.

Beaumont ladies were sent out of town, and their rooms were
rented to oil men willing to pay practically any price for a place
to lay their heads. The Crosby House bar remained the watering
place of the elite, but business was good in all Beaumont's saloons: in 1901 half the whiskey sold in the state of Texas was
consumed in Beaumont.

Then the doctors in Beaumont announced that the water supply, which was mainly rainwater caught in cisterns, had become polluted. The medical profession recommended the use of boiled water or, if that was unavailable, whiskey. Boiled water was soon on sale for a nickle a drink or one dollar a gallon, but this didn't seem to cut into the sale of whiskey at all.

It was natural, too, that men who were gambling all day on oil would gamble a little at night for recreation. There were gambling halls all over town and in most of the hotel rooms. It was far more profitable to let out a room to a group of sportsmen in exchange for a percentage of the pot than it was to rent rooms to people just to sleep in, even if eight and ten and more people in the same room became the rule of the land.

And the outright fakes and charlatans arrived and set up business. A fortune teller named Madame LaMonte took a room in the Cordova Hotel and began to offer advice (at ten dollars a crack) on which oil stocks to buy and which to sell. Within a month, she offered to buy the hotel. Within two months, however, some of her advice had failed to pay off, and she left town (with two valises full of cash) just ahead of the party armed with a rail, several buckets of tar, and a pillow full of feathers.

Somewhat more imaginative than Madame LaMonte was George Fenley of Uvalde, Texas, who arrived in Beaumont to announce that he had X-ray eyes and would, for a price, inform anyone who asked him where oil could be found one thousand feet or so beneath the surface.

With a perfectly straight face he pointed at the earth in one spot and said that if a well were drilled there, oil would be found at 1,100 feet. The well was dug and oil found, and Fenley's price rose astronomically. Nobody seemed to recall that *all* the oil found so far had been found at about 1,100 feet.

One of the smartest deals pulled was perfectly legal. Higgins's original Gladys City Corporation was still in existence. Colonel E. M. House of Austin, Texas (who was later to be a close advisor of President Woodrow Wilson), arrived in town bank-rolled by a group of anonymous Yankees. House went to the Gladys City Corporation and bought the streets and alleys of Gladys City. Since the streets and alleys crisscrossed Spindletop Heights, this gave them land in between everybody else's land. The company was capitalized at $1 million, and the stock was sold out in 36 hours.

Also legal, if somewhat questionable ethically, were the ac-tions of the railroad brakeman who arrived in Beaumont, paid $1.00 for a lease on one-quarter of an acre of unproved land, and then formed a $1 million oil company to exploit it. The company put the brakeman on the payroll as president at $10,000 a month. The company lasted until there was no more money to pay the president, whereupon, after a brief career in oil, he retired from the industry and from the railroad.

Everybody was so busy finding oil or buying leases to look for it or forming companies to do either or both that hardly anyone noticed that dumping all that oil on the market had caused the price of it to drop until it reached five cents a barrel.

chapter 10

STANDARD OIL, WHICH HAD BECOME KNOWN TO its critics as "the octopus," was extending its tenacles toward the Royal Dutch companies in the East Indies. After the annual report to stockholders for the year 1894 was made public, Royal Dutch looked like a good thing to 26 Broadway. The next year, Standard's man in Europe, W. H. Libby, opened talks with Kessler of Royal Dutch. Nothing much came of them, primarily because Standard was in the habit of offering what it felt like paying for something, rather than basing its purchase offer on what the property was actually worth.

Two years later Standard made another offer. This time it proposed that Royal Dutch quadruple its capital (from 3 million shares to 12 million). Standard would buy all of the new shares at 750 florins a share. Since Standard would then control three-quarters of the company, it would operate Royal Dutch as a wholly owned producing, refining, and marketing subsidiary, operating east of Suez. There were several flaws in the offer, the main one being that the Royal Dutch company valued each share at 4,500 florins, 6 times what Standard was offering. Standard's offer was rejected.

The next round came after the price of Royal Dutch shares on the Amsterdam market dropped to about 2,250 florins in the latter part of 1897. This was still 3 times what Standard had offered to pay for them, but Royal Dutch officers learned that Standard was quietly buying all the shares it could at 2,250 florins a share. There was a hasty meeting of the board of directors of Royal Dutch and a quick public announcement of some new bylaws.

Royal Dutch issued 1,500 shares of preferred stock. The Royal Dutch preferred would have all the voting power. Furthermore, it could not be sold without the permission of the other holders of Royal Dutch preferred. Most important, it could be sold only to loyal subjects of the Dutch Crown or to corporations whose officers were loyal subjects of the Dutch crown.

Standard just coiled up its tentacles and went elsewhere. Since the company controlled all the American oil business and had interests elsewhere, it could afford to bide its time.

When the new century began, Royal Dutch's competition in Asia included the Shell Transport & Trading Company, Ltd., of London. Shell was a little larger, but its business wasn't limited to oil, and it had been in business in Asia for a long time. The firm's founder, Marcus Samuel, had started out in 1830 exporting the machine-made products of England to Asia and importing raw materials, including polished seashells, tea, jute, rice, and copra (split coconut shells). The Shell Transport & Trading Company, Ltd., had a much nicer ring to it than, for example, the Jute Transport & Trading Company, Ltd., and Shell it became, first by word of mouth and then officially.

Samuel became an expert in shipping, rather than a merchant. He made his money by careful routing of ships, most of which he had chartered, so that his shipping costs provided his margin of profit, rather than the profit he made by swapping, for example, an English piano or five hundred yards of English woven material for so much jute or rice or seashells.

Twenty-three years after Marcus Samuel went in business, Commodore Matthew Perry of the United States Navy landed in

Japan and opened up the Japanese islands to trade. The Japanese underwent a massive shakeup of ancient custom and then became good traders, which they still are.

In 1874 Marcus Samuel died, and the business came into the hands of his two sons, Marcus Samuel and Samuel Samuel. The company had been drifting more and more into the transport aspect of its business, and when the brothers started looking for something they could transport at a profit, they realized that Japan was about to become a large customer for kerosene, which the Japanese couldn't produce themselves.

Since they were Europeans, the Samuels quite naturally turned to a European source of oil, rather than dealing with Americans. The younger Marcus Samuel went to the Russian oil fields in Baku in 1890. When he got there, he found the Nobel brothers already on the scene. (These were Robert and Ludvig Nobel, older brothers of Alfred Nobel.) They had been doing business in Baku since the 1870s.

The Baku fields are on the land-locked Caspian Sea. The Nobels had been refining the Baku crude, sending it by ship up the Volga River, and selling it in the Russian interior. (The czar was getting a percentage, since he owned the field.)

While there was oil in the region, there was no wood or, at least, not in the quantities that existed in Asia or the United States. It was financially impossible to make wooden barrels and crates in which to ship the Russian oil, a problem the Nobel brothers solved by designing the first modern oil tanker. The Nobel vessel used the double-walled hull of the ship itself as the oil container, where previously oil tanks had been installed inside holds. To reduce the danger of fire, they moved all the working parts of the ship (in particular the boilers) aft. Present-day tankers are built on the same principles of design.

There was no shipyard on the Caspian Sea, so the first tanker, named the *Zoroaster* after the religion based on a fire in ancient times at the Baku field, was laid down and built (but not launched) in Sweden. Once it was built, it was cut in sections, loaded on barges, and floated to the Caspian Sea over the inland waterways of Russia.

During the 1880s a railroad, the *Transcaucasian & Black Sea*, was formed to connect Baku with Batum on the Black Sea. The founders went broke when construction had gone just far enough to interest the Paris branch of the Rothschild banking family. The Rothschilds provided the money to finish the line and buy rolling stock and took control of it. Since the main function of the railroad was the transportation of petroleum and petroleum products, the Rothschilds went into the oil business, too.

They formed the Commercial and Industrial Society of Caspian and Black Sea Naptha. For reasons not quite clear, this company came to be known as "Bnito." In any event the Rothschild funds saw the railroad completed in 1883, and Bnito was soon selling Baku kerosene refined in a Bnito refinery in continental Europe and in England.

When Marcus Samuel saw the Rothschild operation and the Nobel tankers he felt right at home. If he had a Nobel-style tanker and could buy Rothschild kerosene, he could haul the kerosene cheaply through the newly opened Suez Canal and undersell the Rockefellers in Asia. The Rothschilds weren't greedy. They agreed to sell Samuel what kerosene he wanted at a good price, providing he sold it east of Suez.

That left the problem of a tanker. The Samuel family had a splendid reputation in England, and there was at the time a shortage of work for British shipyards. William Gray & Sons, shipbuilders of West Hartlepool, agreed to build a tanker for the Samuel brothers to be paid for out of their profits. The 4,200 ton *Murex* was launched in May 1892. The Rothschilds obligingly used their considerable influence on the Suez Canal Company (in which they were individual stockholders and to which, as a banking firm, they had loaned enormous amounts of money) to have the rules against transporting petroleum through the canal locks suspended.

When the *Murex* nosed away from the Suez Canal for the first time in the summer of 1892, loaded with a cargo of bulk kerosene for the Orient, it marked the end of Rockefeller domination of the Asiatic petroleum market.

The Samuel brothers knew shipping, and they knew the Asiatic market. Their plan was to ship kerosene in bulk to major depots at seaports in India, Malaya, and along the China coast. There it would be pumped into bulk storage tanks. From the major depots, the kerosene would be transported, still in bulk, by railroad tank car and barge and smaller tankers to smaller depots in the interior. The smaller depots would put the kerosene in drums for shipment to retailers. The retailers would put the kerosene into the buyers' own containers and then return the drums to the depots for refilling.

The tank farms at major and small depots would be built by local businessmen, which would involve these colonial entrepreneurs and thus inspire them to sell the Samuel brothers' kerosene, rather than Standard Oil's. It would also have the second benefit of ending the Samuel brothers' responsibility for the oil as soon as possible. As soon as the oil was pumped out of the *Murex*, it belonged to the local businessmen.

It was a splendid plan, but it didn't take into consideration differences between Eastern and Western thinking. A five-gallon kerosene tin to the Europeans was simply a tin can, of some value at one time to contain kerosene and practically useless when emptied. To the Asians, however, the five-gallon tin cans were far more. Once emptied, they could be converted into cooking utensils, wash basins, and roofing material.

When the Samuels realized that the Asian consumers wanted the tin cans, as well as the kerosene they contained, they changed their distribution plans. Instead of having the subdepots put the kerosene into drums, they put it into five-gallon cans

Not all the oil sold in Africa is dispensed from drums. This is a modern station in Nairobi, Kenya. MOBIL OIL PHOTO.

made on the spot. This solved several problems neatly. It permitted the bulk shipment of kerosene over most of the transportation route. It eliminated the cost of drums and of shipping the drums back from the interior when emptied, and, an important sales point, it provided the Asiatic customer with a brand new tin can in much better shape than Standard Oil's tin cans, which were rusty and battered after their long sea trip from the United States.

(This problem of containers is still with the oil business. Arnold Hartpence, a Montanan who spent his career in the African oil trade and who retired as president of Mobil Oil, Congo, told me that as late as 1968 he was having tin-can problems. His superiors in the United States had eliminated the five-gallon tin can because of leakage problems, substituting more substantial steel drums, which were supposed to be returned like soft-drink bottles for refilling. A deposit was to be charged to make their return worthwhile. It didn't work. Despite the deposit charged, the Congolese in the interior refused to believe that the containers were to be returned. Since they couldn't use the heavier steel as they used the light tin of the cans, the empty drums were obviously useless and were discarded where emptied. So far as the Congolese were concerned, the deposit charged meant that Mobil had raised the price of its kerosene and gasoline, and they transferred their business to other companies who not only sold their products cheaper but threw in a usable tin can as well. It took all of Hartpence's considerable powers of persuasion to get this point across in the boardrooms of New York City.)

In the mid-1890s, the czar of Russia began to make threatening noises about his oil fields. If the Nobels and the Rothschilds were making money paying him a percentage, didn't it stand to reason that he could make more money by taking over the oil fields, the distillery, and the railroad himself? The czar struck first at the Nobels with an imperial decree that any oil transported from Batum to Vladivostok must be carried in Russian ships.

The Samuel brothers reasoned that the next thing the czar was likely to do was shut off the sale of petroleum to them and transport his Russian petroleum in his Russian ships, to Asia, which would leave them with nothing but a fleet of heavily mortgaged tankers. In 1896 the Samuels went into the oil-production business with the purchase of a small field on the island of Koetei on the shores of East Borneo. They began to erect a refinery at Balik Papan.

The Shell Transport & trading Company, separate from M. Samuel & Sons, took over the tankers, the oil fields, the projected refinery, and the tank farms at the depots and subdepots. Stock in Shell was given in proportion to the value of the tank farms and other installations, but the Samuel brothers made sure they still held unquestionable control of the business.

By 1901 this method of doing business had proven to be a good one. The Samuel brothers received a visit from a representative of Standard Oil, who announced that if the price were right, Standard might be willing to take the business off their hands. With British reserve, the Standard representative was turned down. Standard then began its usual practice of cutting prices, selling its own products at a loss, if necessary, to get the business and drive its competition out of the marketplace.

It was doing the same thing to Royal Dutch, of course, and the idea of merging the two (smaller by far) companies occurred to both Deterding of Royal Dutch and Marcus Samuel as early as the late 1890s. But Shell was as much larger than Royal Dutch as Standard was larger than both and moved in higher circles. Marcus Samuel was at the time lord mayor of London and an intimate of the royal family. Deterding decided that while Samuel might be interested in getting together with Royal Dutch, he would probably want to buy them out, which Deterding didn't want to happen.

The first thing he did was to establish a producer's association of the other small Dutch East Indies companies, so they could speak with one voice and more or less with one bank account. Then Spindletop came in, and Samuel was quick to make a deal with the Guffey Petroleum Company for large quantities of oil over a long period of time. His contract with Bnito forbade him to sell Baku field petroleum in Europe, but there was no prohibition on selling Texas oil in Europe. Shell signed a contract calling for four tankers, the largest yet built, to haul Spindletop production from Texas to Europe.

On the surface, Shell looked tremendous. From the 1 tanker in 1892 the fleet had grown to 30 ocean-going tankers by 1900, and more were being built. There were 31 ocean depots (the tank farms into which the tankers unloaded their cargos) in the Far East and 11 more were either under construction or planned. There were 310 subdepots throughout Asia, an oil field in Sumatra complete with new refinery, and, in addition to the contract for oil from Texas, Shell had Bnito in Batum and

Sumatran producers under contract for both crude oil and refinery products. It had, in fact, more widely spread sources of
supply than did Standard Oil. Despite its size and obvious potential for profit, however, Shell paid dividends of only 2.5 percent
for 1901. Royal Dutch shareholders got 24 percent dividends.

This gave Deterding of Royal Dutch the courage to proceed
with his affiliation ideas. He knew an Englishman, a ship char-
terer named Frederick Lane, well enough to ask him to act as a
mediary with Samuel. The Samuel brothers and Lane knew each
other well, so the one real problem was personality. Marcus
Samuel was an important man, long used to giving orders and
not at all accustomed to taking suggestions, much less orders,
from anyone else. Deterding was much the same kind of man,
who wrote of himself at the time, "Mine is a personality which
does not readily submerge itself."

The two strong-willed men finally met face to face while their
friends held their breath. The meeting didn't last long at all, and
while (not being the kind of men to do that sort of thing) Samuel and Deterding did not emerge from the meeting room with
their arms around each other, they did announce with great
dignity that they had found a solution.

An official agreement was signed on June 27, 1902, establishing the Asiatic Petroleum Company, Ltd. There were three partners, Samuel (the Shell Transport & Trading Company), Deterding (Royal Dutch), and the Rothschilds. Samuel became
chairman of the board of the new company. Deterding was
named general manager.*

---

* The term "general manager" in European circles corresponds to
"president" in American business. Since Europeans think of the title
"president" primarily in political terms, and Americans think that
people called "general managers" manage nothing more important
than the office stationery and a squad of file clerks, this still leads to
wholesale confusion whenever European and American business
executives get together and exchange titles.

It is important to understand that the Asiatic Petroleum Company did not absorb any of the assets of Shell or Royal Dutch or anyone else. It was simply a company formed to take advantage of the collective assets of its owners. Royal Dutch, Shell, and Bnito kept their production facilities but turned over their Asiatic marketing (only) to Asiatic. The tankers, railroad tankers, and tank farms which soon blossomed in Asiatic Petroleum Company colors were actually just rented from Shell or Royal Dutch or Bnito on a ten-year lease.

The new company accomplished several things. It guaranteed a source of supply of petroleum products for Asia, which kept the czar and/or Standard Oil from putting the three companies out of business one at a time. It provided a more efficient distribution system, because it did away with the duplication that had previously existed when the companies operated independently. And in unity there was strength.

The new company, in other words, could have given Standard a good fight, one that would keep the octopus from gobbling them up, but it stood no chance of beating Standard Oil. To dislodge Standard from its position on top of the hill would take a revolution. Spindletop was spectacular, but it wasn't quite enough.

The revolution wasn't long in coming. It was, in fact, already under way even before Spindletop: Charles E. Duryea and his brother Frank produced the first American-built automobile in 1892, and by 1895 they had a factory in operation in Chicopee Falls, Massachusetts, producing what they called the "Duryea buggyaut."

In Kokomo, Indiana, Elwood Haynes, who was the field superintendent of a natural gas company, got together with one of the company's mechanics, Elmer Apperson, and made an automobile which was the hit of the 1894 Kokomo Fourth of July celebration and parade.

Henry Ford, who was then the chief engineer of the Detroit

Gas Light Company (now Detroit Edison), was already experimenting with automobiles in a brick building behind his house to the consternation of his employers, who felt that fooling around with something so obviously impractical was beneath the dignity of one of their senior employees.

In 1900 Ransom E. Olds moved from Lansing, Michigan, where for 3 years he'd been building cars, to Detroit, where he started mass-producing cars for the first time. In 2 years he built 2,000 Oldsmobiles, sold them for $650 each, and returned a cash dividend of 105 percent to the people who had invested in his company.

In the same year that Asiatic Petroleum was organized, the Ford Motor Company as it is known today was organized. There had been several other companies involving Ford and his name. One of them was called the Henry Ford Company, although the majority stockholder had been Henry M. Leland of Faulconer & Leland, the largest machine shop in the United States. When Ford and Leland disagreed, Leland bought out Ford, and part of the price was his agreement not to use Ford's name on any more cars. Leland considered calling his cars Lelands but decided he needed a name with more class. He settled on the name of a French explorer who had roamed the area several hundred years before for the king of France—Cadillac.

In 1895 there had been 300 automobiles in all of America. Ten years later, there were 78,000. Five years later, in 1910, there were 459,000, and by 1914, there were 1,700,000. Each of them, of course, came equipped with a gas tank, which had to be periodically filled.

chapter 11

UNTIL THE AUTOMOBILE BROUGHT WITH IT A DE-
mand for gasoline, gasoline was not really an important part of
the petroleum industry. Some gasoline occurs naturally (well,
or casing head gasoline), and it always occurs whenever petroleum is refined. But until there was a market for it, it was considered a nuisance. It was too explosive to be used in lanterns,
for example, and countless billions of gallons of gasoline were
diverted from well heads and refineries to open pits and burned,
just to get rid of it. At one time the federal government assigned inspectors to refineries to make sure unscrupulous refiners
didn't sneak it into kerosene for sale to the public.

At this point in the story of oil, we should consider just what
is petroleum, this substance that was making people rich as
Croesus, this substance that changed, for the better, the life of
every human being on planet Earth.

There are thousands of different chemicals in the crude oil
that flows from beneath the earth's surface. They range from
extremely light gases to semisolid materials composed mainly of
carbon (for example, asphalt and paraffin wax).

Some crude oils weigh as little as 6.5 pounds a gallon, and
some weigh nearly as much as water (8.33 pounds per gallon).
Some crude is as thick and black as melted tar, and other crude
is thin, colorless, and as fluid as water.

Crude oil is composed largely of hydrocarbons, mixtures of hydrogen and carbon in various proportions. Refining crude oil is the process by which the natural, or crude, oil is broken down into the products people can use, as the outline below illustrates.

Petroleum consists of liquids, gases, and solids, from which people take:

1. Solids
    a. Fuel (coke and briquettes)
    b. Lubricants (greases and graphite)
    c. Industrial products (asphalt, carbon, waxes, and rust preventatives)
2. Gases
    a. Fuel (natural gas)
    b. Organic chemicals (fertilizers and so on)
3. Liquids
    a. Fuels (liquid petroleum gases [LPG], jet fuel, gasoline, diesel fuel, kerosene, and fuel oil)
    b. Lubricants (motor oil and industrial oils and greases)
    c. Industrial Products (insecticides, munitions, absorption oils, organic chemicals, polishes, wood preservatives, coolants, power transmission oils, quenching oils, plasticizers, cleaners, solvents, medicinal oils, rust preventatives, and insulating oil)

Almost from the beginning people understood that petroleum was a combination of things rather than an element. Even the ancients understood that their bitumen, which they used as a glue and paving material, was what was left after other portions, or fractions, of crude oil had dissipated into the air.

The various hydrocarbon fractions of petroleum have different boiling points, some of them as low as normal temperatures, some even lower (they will "boil" away at normal temperature and vaporize), and some very high.

The first intentional refining of petroleum (which remains the first step in refining today) was simply the boiling of crude oil under controlled conditions so that its components could be separated. Since the boiling point of hydrocarbon compounds depends on the size of their molecules, the separation also results in separation by hydrocarbon size.

A fractionating tower isn't nearly as complicated as it sounds. It consists of a tall, sealed vessel with a number of floors inside. Each floor is perforated with pipes equipped with bubble caps. A bubble cap is a simple device (similar to that used by home wine makers) which fits over a pipe. Normally, the bubble cap seals the pipe closed. When there is pressure from below, the bubble cap will lift, permitting the gas to escape from below. When the pressure is gone, the bubble cap falls by gravity back over the hole, sealing it and keeping the gas from going back down the pipe.

Crude oil is heated to seven hundred or eight hundred degrees Fahrenheit (depending on its specific gravity—the higher the gravity, the higher the temperature) and pumped into the fractionating tower at the level of the eighth or ninth floor. (There are from twenty to forty floors, depending on the design of the tower). As soon as the pumping pressure is relieved, the crude oil vaporizes. The vapors rise through the tower, cooling as they rise according to the laws of physics and because they are no longer being heated and are cooling naturally.

Some of the vaporized crude oil, the heavier fractions, doesn't get very far before its temperature drops below its boiling point and it becomes a liquid again. The really heavy crude, that portion which will become asphalt, for example, is very thick and cools very quickly, because the lighter fractions have vaporized. For this reason the bottom floors of the tower have to be heated with steam to keep it liquid so that it can flow out of the tower.

As the rest of the vaporized crude rises floor by floor through the fractionating tower, first the temperature of the fractions with the consistency of lubricating oil drops below the boiling

Catalytic fractionating towers at Gulf Oil's Alliance Refinery on the Mississippi River near New Orleans. GULF OIL PHOTO.

point, and these fractions condense into lubricating oil, which flows out of the tower to lubricating oil storage tanks. The lighter fractions continue to rise through bubble caps. A little higher up the tower, the temperature cools below the boiling point of fuel oil, and that fraction of the vapor condenses into fuel oil, which is drawn off. Still higher up the tower, the vapor temperature drops below the boiling point of kerosene, and that fraction condenses into kerosene, which is drawn off. Very near the top of the tower, the vapor is entirely gasoline. Some of it condenses naturally into gasoline, which is drawn off like the other fractions. But some gasoline vapors have boiling points lower than normal temperatures (as you can see when the gas station attendant spills gasoline on the ground and it evaporates, boils away, almost immediately).

These vapors are put through a condenser and chilled. The gasoline vapors which can be condensed are added to the other gasoline fractions. Some of the gaseous gas is used for other purposes, and some is simply burned. Anyone who has ever seen a refinery at night has seen the shooting flames of fire burning brilliantly. The gas burned is so volatile that it can't be mixed with anything else, and burning it is the only safe way to get rid of it; it can't be used even for its heat. If the oil industry could figure out anything to do with it—and they've been trying since Oil Creek—they wouldn't burn it.

In the Pennsylvania and California and Texas fields, in Baku and Sumatra, and elsewhere in the first years of this century, gasoline was taken directly from the top layers of the fractionating towers and burned, because no one knew what to do with it. There was no demand for it at all; it was a useless by-product.

What people wanted was kerosene. Kerosene could be used to light lamps and heat stoves. The heavier fractions had some uses as lubricants and greases and as wax for paraffin candles, and the really heavy fractions, the asphalts, were coming into use as paving and roofing materials.

The automobile (and, in the first couple of years, gasoline-powered stationary engines used to generate power and light) changed all this. Gasoline became the most wanted product of crude oil, not an unwelcome by-product. Even in Asia as early as 1903, Standard Oil contracted with Asiatic to buy all the gasoline Asiatic could sell them. In the United States the demand for gasoline was such that Standard found itself with quantities of kerosene on hand, and the American market was saturated with kerosene. Standard's solution to the problem was to dump it on the European market for whatever it would bring. Whatever money it made was better than no money at all. The European consumer, of course, got a bargain. But somebody had to get hurt, and this time it was Samuel. When Shell joined Royal Dutch, Samuel kept his European market. In 1904 Shell sold 35 million gallons of kerosene in Europe, and lost $545,440 doing so.

Samuel was also having other troubles with America. In the flush days of Spindletop, he had contracted with Guffey to buy vast quantities of oil (4,500,000 barrels a year) for 20 years at 25 cents a barrel.

The J. M. Guffey, built in 1902 to ship Spindletop oil to England. GULF OIL PHOTO.

It looked like a mutually satisfying deal. Samuel could well afford to pay a quarter a barrel, and Guffey could make a nice profit selling it, since oil was then available in apparently unlimited quantities at a dime a barrel.

And then Spindletop production fell off, and the price to Guffey was thirty cents a barrel; he would lose a nickle on each barrel. W. L. Mellon put the problem in Andrew Mellon's lap. Andrew Mellon went to London and had a long, private talk with Samuel. Samuel's legal position was iron-clad, but he released Guffey (and the Mellons as well) from their obligation to provide him with oil.

The Texas Company was also having trouble with Spindletop. By the end of 1902 Texaco had gone into the fuel oil market in a large way. In nearby Louisiana, sugar plantations were burning 450,000 tons of coal a year to power their mills. The plantation and mill owners could get as much energy from 1,350,000 barrels of oil. Oil was a better fuel, there were no ashes to be hauled away after it had been burned, and at a price of $1.00 a barrel delivered, it would be cheaper.

The Texas Company agreed to pay its affiliate a quarter a barrel for oil, and to take its profits from what was left after the costs of refining and transportation to Louisiana. To make good on its promise to deliver oil, the Texas Company bought 15 acres on Spindletop, on which were a number of producing wells, and contracted for 6 more wells to be drilled at $6,000 each. And then, in the fall of 1902, Spindletop production plummeted almost overnight from 62,000 barrels a day to 20,000. A year later, it was down to 5,000 barrels a day.

Cullinan, the driving force behind The Texas Company, had taken an option on 865 acres of land at Sour Lake, 20-odd miles from the Spindletop field, paying $20,000 for the option to buy it later for $1 million. Part of the option deal required that 3 test wells be drilled on the property. (In case the option was exercised because oil was found, the original owners would be paid a royalty.) When the first salt water began to appear in Spindletop wells, Cullinan ordered the first Sour Lake well drilled. He found some oil, not enough to cause much enthusiasm, but enough to make drilling a second well seem wise. The second well also yielded oil in about the same quantities, and a third was put down. On January 8, 1903, Sour Lake gushed in.

It was time to exercise the option to buy the property at $1 million. That was the businesslike thing to do, but there was one problem: the Texas Company didn't have a million dollars in cash or anything like it. John W. "Bet-a-Million" Gates came to the rescue and lived up to his name. He first announced that he would take $590,000 worth of new stock the Texas Company was going to sell to raise the million. Having done that, he said, "I'll go for the whole million, if you can't find it elsewhere."

It wasn't necessary to take Gates up on his offer. The stock subscription was sold out, and some fancy talking by Texas Company lawyers about an unclear title to the land got the price down to $900,000. The Texas company owned the new field and had $100,000 in the bank. It was the last time they were ever to be concerned about money.

One of the founders and directors of the Texas Company was a taciturn German named Arnold Schlaet, who had little to do with field operations of the company. He interested himself in raising money for the company and selling its products. He worked out of a small office in New York City and transacted most business with Texas over the telegraph lines. To save words the Texas Company was abbreviated to "Texaco." Inevitably, people stopped using the Texas Company name, and Texaco it became, first popularly, then on the labels of its products, and finally on its official corporate stationery.

Texaco's business philosophy, in large measure the business philosophy of Arnold Schlaet, was based on the simple idea that it made good sense to make use of every possible by-product in a gallon of crude oil. It adapted the unofficial slogan of the Chicago stockyards (we use every part of the pig but the squeal) to the oil business. It next began to court the business of the ultimate consumer.

For example, when Texaco entered the kerosene business in Philadelphia, its major competitor was Standard Oil. Standard had owned the market for so long that it sold kerosene at its own convenience: once a week a Standard Oil tank wagon would appear at hardware and grocery stores to fill the retail merchant's tanks. If his tank wasn't large enough to hold the kerosene he needed for a week's sales (or if there happened to be a large demand for kerosene that week), that was too bad. The tank wagon only made weekly calls.

Texaco started by making twice-a-week deliveries. It was

A Gulf horsedrawn kerosene wagon of the period. GULF OIL PHOTO.

charged (and is probably true) that the Texaco tank wagons made their calls the day before the Standard tank wagons were scheduled. The retail merchants' tanks were often empty, and Texaco got the business.

Standard countered by starting its own twice-a-week deliveries, and Texaco responded to that by making daily deliveries. When Standard began making daily deliveries, there wasn't much else Texaco could do to be obliging, but by then it had carved out a market for itself.

Texaco intended to capture and retain the market for gasoline. In the year the company was founded, 1902, there were 23,000 cars on the dirt roads of America. Ten years later there were 902,000 cars and 41,000 trucks. Many of the roads were paved with Texaco asphalt from the lower end of the fractionating towers, and many of the cars were greased and fueled with Texaco lubricating fractions and gasoline. The consumption of lubricating oils in the early days was much higher than it is now. In 1912 the Studebaker Motor Car Company, for example, took a full page ad in major newspapers to announce that one of its cars on an economy run had gone 1,000 miles in 5 200-mile stages averaging 29 miles per gallon of gasoline and 100 miles per quart of oil. The Saxon Motor Car Company rose to the boast with an ad of its own saying that a 1912 Saxon had gone 1,000 miles "over regular roads" and delivered 30 miles per gallon of gas and 150 miles per quart of oil. Standard Oil's standard brand of lubricating oil, "Polarine," which was guaranteed to be "frost and carbon proof," came in no container smaller than a gallon and was most commonly sold in 5-gallon cans with 20- and 42-gallon drums readily available for those interested in economy.

Gasoline sales and methods of selling evolved rapidly and naturally from the early days. The first man to buy gasoline from the Union Oil Company of California was an intrepid motorist named A. D. Williams of Santa Barbara. When he showed up at

The first Gulf service station was built in Pittsburgh, Pennsylvania, in 1912. This photo was taken in 1913. GULF OIL PHOTO.

Gulf's first drive-in service station, built in 1913. GULF OIL PHOTO.

the warehouse to buy a drum of gasoline, he was told to come back in a week as none was on hand.

Gasoline was at first handled like kerosene in barrels, drums, and five-gallon tin cans. Unfortunately, it had a tendency to eat through the lead seals of the tin cans. Early motorists bought it in drums, took it home, and serviced themselves when necessary by decanting the gasoline from the drums into a manageable vessel and then pouring it from that into their tanks.

Automobile engines were more critical than kerosene lamps, however, and bits of dirt and other matter which posed no problems at the bottom of a kerosene lamp did so with cars. Gasoline users quickly learned to pour the gasoline through a filter, usually a piece of chamois.

The next step was for motorists to show up at a petroleum dealer's warehouse, where, if they weren't busy with something more important, workers could be cajoled into dispensing five or ten gallons from warehouse stock. Soon, this habit of motorists reached the point that somebody's nearly full-time services were required just to decant gasoline.

The standard technique then became putting a fifty-gallon drum on a high shelf and inserting a length of garden hose into the bung hole. The first service-station attendant serviced their customers by siphoning gas into their tanks. No customer had the audacity to ask that the attendant check the level of his oil; that was clearly his own responsibility.

Next came the hand pump, already in use to dispense light lubricating oils and only slightly modified to handle gasoline. Soon the gasoline attendant was spending too much time rolling out heavy 55-gallon drums of gasoline to the place where he would dispense it, and an underground tank holding as many as 500 gallons was installed.

Next the pump was improved, emerging as a pole with a glass container on top holding as many as five gallons. The gasoline was pumped from the underground storage tanks into the glass container. When the desired amount of gas had gone into the measuring container, it was fed by gravity from the container into the customer's tank.

On May 1, 1911, the Central Oil Company of Detroit, Michigan, a small jobbing concern, opened the first gasoline filling station with a good deal of fanfare. It was a 20 by 25-foot shelter on a 100 by 150-foot lot on the corner of West Fort and First streets. Central had hired a consulting engineer, F. A. Bean, to design and build a filling station that would solve the problem of dispensing gasoline once and for all. Bean came up with a 1,000-gallon tank and a hand-operated pump, which dispensed gasoline 1 gallon at a time. It was an expensive gamble in an attempt to attract business. The building, driveways, pump, and other equipment cost $1,200.

On its first day of operation it sold about 100 gallons. Six weeks after it opened, sales were up to 200 gallons a day, and 6 months later, the filling station was pouring out 2,000 gallons a day. Before the 6 months were up, however, the first filling station had another distinction, one it would rather have foregone, but one which set a trend which endures today: It was robbed. Central was not discouraged and in the fall of 1911 set up another filling station, thus starting the first chain of service stations in the industry.

What Central was doing quickly came to the attention of the producers and refiners, and in 1912 Gulf built the first company owned filling station (the term "service station" was, like free air, still some time off) at Baum Boulevard and St. Clair Street in Pittsburgh, Pennsylvania.

Soon, filling and service stations sprouted up all over America, ever more elaborate proof that from 1911 onward gasoline was the largest and most profitable facet of the oil industry.

chapter 12

THE DEMAND FOR OIL CONTINUED TO GROW AS people found more practical uses for it. In February 1912 the Danish 4,950-gross-ton *Selandia,* the first diesel-powered ocean liner, made her maiden voyage from Copenhagen to Bangkok. On May 17, 1912, the Liquid Petroleum Gas (LPG) industry was born when tanks were installed on the farm of John W. Gahring, in Waterford, Pennsylvania. Gahring used the gas for heating his house and workshop.

In October, the Roxanna Petroleum Company was organized. It was the wedge with which the Royal Dutch-Shell group entered the American market. It didn't attract much public attention, because most of it was focused on Congress and on the state legislatures, which were in the process of ratifying the 16th Admendment to the Constitution. Despite howls of rage from the citizens, the politicians had their way and the federal income tax became law in February 1913.

The next month the British Royal Navy, the largest in the world, announced that it would immediately begin to build vessels using oil for fuel and to convert what coal burners it could to the use of petroleum.

In September 1913 the Panama Canal was completed, permitting for the first time water-borne shipments from the Atlantic to the Pacific to cross the narrow neck of land connecting North and South America instead of making the lengthy, often hazardous journey around the tip of South America.

World War I started on August 1, 1914, with the declaration of war by Germany against Russia, followed on August 3 by the German declaration of war against France. The war went well at first for the Germans, and by September 6 they were threatening Paris from positions near the Marne River. The automobile went to war for the first time when the military governor of Paris, General Joseph Gallieni, commandeered all the taxis, trucks, and private automobiles he could get his hands on and used them to rush French reinforcements from the capital to the battle. "The taxicab army" is credited with saving Paris and thus affecting the eventual outcome of the war.

Americans were outraged on May 7, 1914, when the British passenger liner *Lusitania* was sunk by a German submarine and 139 Americans died, but there was just as much outrage in September, when a tank car holding 10,000 gallons of "casing head" (natural) gasoline blew up at Ardmore, Oklahoma, killing 43 and injuring 500. The attitude of many people seemed to be that if you sailed on a ship belonging to a belligerent in a war, you got what you deserved. The exploding tank car was something else again. There was a large public outcry, resulting in many safety regulations being forced on the oil industry.

In October 1914 the United States began construction of the Lincoln Highway, an ambitious undertaking which would link both coasts of the United States.

There was a good deal of public interest, too, in the announcement made toward the end of 1915 by the Standard Oil Company of New Jersey that henceforth the work week for its employees, with no loss in pay, would be cut from seven nine-hour days to six eight-hour days.

In April 1916 a man named Harry Sinclair went into the oil

The U.S.S. Maumee had long service with the navy. Here she is shown in 1942, painted in preradar camouflage. U.S. NAVY PHOTO.

This young midshipman was to become Fleet Admiral Chester W. Nimitz, who commanded the largest fleet ever assembled by the United States or any other navy. COURTESY FLEET ADMIRAL NIMITZ, FROM THE U.S. NAVY.

business with the formation of the Service Pipe Line Company of Maine. A good deal more was to be heard of Mr. Sinclair.

On September 15, 1916, a strange vehicle based on a caterpillar tractor (an American invention, made possible by the internal combustion engine) rolled out of the fog in France, crossed No-Man's Land, and breached the German trenches. The Germans set up an indignant howl. This tank was obviously the most uncivilized weapon of war ever employed. It was also invincible. The Germans immediately began making tanks for themselves.

Later the same year, the U.S.S. *Maumee*, a tanker, was commissioned. She was the first United States Navy vessel to be powered by diesel engines. The engines were the pride and joy of a young lieutenant named Chester W. Nimitz. (In World War II Nimitz became one of the very few five-star fleet admirals the navy has ever had.)

On April 6, 1917, the United States entered World War I. Two months later, two more new oil companies were started, The Phillips Petroleum Company (on June 13) and the Humble Oil & Refining Company (on June 21). In Texas, a small supply company called the Hughes Tool Company offered for rent (not sale) a patented drilling bit, far superior to anything else on the market and for which great things were predicted.

In Russia, one of the first acts of the Communist government which overthrew (and murdered, together with his family) the Czar was the confiscation of all privately owned oil properties within what was now the Union of Soviet Socialist Republics. With few exceptions oil-producing properties had been held in the name of the Czar and leased to Russian businessmen (or foreigners) on a royalty (concession) basis. The Royal Dutch-Shell group was the largest foreign operator of oil-producing, refining, and transportation facilities and suffered enormous financial loss when its investment was confiscated without any compensation.

As an indication of how much gasoline was being consumed, the government reported in October that 60 million gallons of gasoline were "saved" in 7 weeks when people responded to a government request not to use gas on Sunday. The program wasn't compulsory and applied only to the United States east of the Mississippi. (Sixty million gallons is just under 150,000 barrels. Daily gasoline consumption in 1972 averaged 5,828,571 barrels—242,857 barrels or 10,199,999 gallons per hour.)

The program seemed to be a little late to be truly effective; World War I ended on November 11, 1918, and the military demand for petroleum ended with it. At a banquet in London the next month, Lord Curzon of the British government paid tribute where it was due. "American oil," he said, "and hardly any other, made up that 'wave of petroleum' on which the war was won."

During the war, the airplane had stopped being a curiosity (in Russia Igor Sikorsky had built a four-engine bomber carrying a crew of eleven) and had become a practical tool of transport. Congress set up in December 1918 the first air mail route (New York-Philadelphia-Washington).

The search for more oil continued to grow, too. With the major companies controlling oil exploration in the United States, two Americans, Mike Benedum and Joe Trees, went elsewhere. Operating with cheap, old-fashioned, and well-worn equipment, they put down a well in the middle of a tropical rain forest in Colombia. At 80 feet they found oil, a small well producing 50 barrels a day. On the strength of this discovery they pushed the drill deeper into the earth. On April 26, 1918, their first well came in again at 2,260 feet, flowing 5,000 barrels a day. Before the year was over, they had put down 2 more wells, and each of them came in with a greater flow than the first. They were back in the United States in early 1919 with $33 million between them.

In February 1919 the politicians in Oregon were the first to see unlimited funds in the oil business, and they decreed the first state tax (a penny a gallon) on gasoline, despite protests from citizens and the oil men alike.

In September and October 1919 three more now-familiar names entered the oil business. In September the Sinclair Oil Company was organized and in October Skelly Oil Company and Murphy Oil Company started up.

In February 1920 oil-connected corruption at the highest echelons of government began with the passage of the Oil Land Leasing Bill. This bill gave the secretary of the interior the right to lease public lands to oil men. The Naval Reserve Oil Lands (designed to insure the navy would always have oil for its ships) were for the moment left under the control of the secretary of the navy. By June, however, the Congress granted the secretary of the navy the power to use his discretion in selling leases or oil or gas itself, from the naval reserves in exchange for other products the navy might need.

This sounded fine to the oil men, and the honeymoon between

Josephus Daniels, secretary of the navy, March 1913–1921.
U.S. NAVY.

*The latest word in delivery trucks to fuel the nation's 9,239,161
motor vehicles was this White-built Gulf truck in 1920.*
GULF OIL PHOTO.

the oil industry and the navy lasted until December, when Navy
Secretary Josephus Daniels said at a banquet in Washington that
the obvious thing to do with all of the nation's oil reserves was to
nationalize them. The honeymoon was over. By the end of 1920
there were 9,239,161 motor vehicles (trucks, buses, and cars)
registered in the United States.

Regardless of Secretary of the Navy Daniels's ideas about
nationalizing the nation's oil, he was an honest man, who would
stand for no hanky-panky with the navy's Teapot Dome and Elk
Hill oil reserves. On May 31, 1921, President Harding solved
this problem neatly by transferring (by executive order, Congress wasn't asked) the naval petroleum reserves from the control of the navy (that is, Daniels) to that of the secretary of the
interior, Albert B. Fall. Fall, who had been born in Kentucky,

was a self-taught lawyer who moved to New Mexico, entered politics, and was elected to the United States Senate in 1912. Reelected in 1918, he was appointed secretary of the interior by Harding shortly before Harding transferred control of the navy's oil reserves to him.

On April 18, 1922, the government (as represented by the Department of the Interior) leased part of the naval oil reserves at Teapot Dome, Wyoming, to private interests. The private interests announced that they expected to start getting the oil out of the ground immediately.

Senator Robert LaFollette of Wisconsin, one of the most unusual senators of all time (depending on whom you asked, he was either one of America's greatest statesmen or a flaming socialist; history suggests he was a little of both) was not caught up in the all-around feeling of joy. Three days after the leases were announced, he introduced a resolution in the Senate calling for the Department of the Interior to release all the facts about the leases at Teapot Dome, Wyoming, and Elk Hills, California, to the Senate. It was a scandal unlike any before and few since. It took the Senate until October of 1923, more than a year later, to begin the actual hearings, but once they were started, a fascinating story developed.

Three areas had been set aside for the navy's petroleum reserve. Reserve No. 1 consisted of 38,000 acres at Elk Hills, California. It had been set aside in 1912. Reserve No. 2, also set aside in 1912, consisted of 30,000 acres in Buena Vista Hills, California. Reserve No. 3 was the 9,321-acre site called Teapot Dome in Wyoming.

Shortly after President Harding transferred control of the reserves to Secretary Fall, Fall entered into secret negotiations with Harry F. Sinclair. On April 7, 1922, the Department of the Interior, without taking bids, gave Sinclair an exclusive contract to take the oil from the Teapot Dome reserve. (This was made public only on April 18.) During 1921 and 1922 Fall secretly leased the two California reserves to Edward Doheny's Pan American Oil Company.

Senator Thomas J. Walsh of Montana, chairman of the investigating committee, quickly learned that Fall and members of his family had, shortly after the leases were granted, received $200,000 in liberty bonds (the World War I version of United States Savings Bonds) from "unknown sources." Secretary Fall was also very popular with Mr. Doheny, who "loaned" him $100,000 in cash without even bothering to get an IOU.

The first public figure to be implicated with Fall was Secretary of the Navy Denby, who resigned his office "for personal reasons." He was replaced by Judge Curtis D. Wilbur of California, who promptly reviewed the navy's files and turned over what he found to the Senate committee. Attorney-General Harry M. Daugherty, whose function it was to protect the United States from crooks in and out of the government, refused to give the senators access to his files, which included those of the bureau which preceded the FBI.

On February 8, 1924, the Congress in a joint resolution announced that on the evidence it was perfectly clear that the contracts Fall had negotiated with Sinclair and Doheny were "executed under circumstances indicating fraud and corruption; without authority on the part of the officers purporting to act for the United States; and in defiance of the policy to maintain in the ground a great reserve supply of oil adequate to the needs of the Navy."

President Harding died after a short illness on August 2, 1923, and Vice-President Calvin Coolidge assumed the office. Coolidge demanded Attorney-General Daugherty's resignation on March 28, 1924. Criminal action was begun against him and against Doheny and Fall, but there was a noticeable lack of enthusiasm to prosecute on the part of President Coolidge, who announced he was "neutral" and personally felt this wasn't any of the president's business.

For an advertising photo, this was hard to beat: Charles
Augustus Lindbergh pouring "Mobiloil B" into the engine of
The Spirit of Saint Louis *just before taking off for Europe.*
MOBIL OIL PHOTO.

Judge Harlan F. Stone of New York replaced Daugherty as attorney-general. Stone's honesty was beyond question, but once he showed a tendency to be as outraged about the matter as most taxpayers, he was promoted out of the attorney-generalship and appointed to the Supreme Court, where he served many years with great distinction. He was replaced as attorney-general by John G. Sargent of Vermont.

The joint resolution of the Congress had also ordered the president to cancel the leases and to bring legal action against anybody who might have broken the law in the matter. This prosecution took a long time, was fought through the courts, and in the end seemed hardly more than a slap on the wrist. Daugherty wasn't even prosecuted. Doheny (for whom Doheny Drive in Los Angeles is named) was turned loose. Harry F. Sinclair was sentenced to and served three months in jail and was fined $500. Immediately on his release he was unanimously "and with acclamation" "reelected" to the presidency of Mammoth Oil Company and voted a bonus.

Secretary Fall was sentenced to a year and a day in jail, and he served it. A year and a day behind bars made him a convicted felon, ineligible for any office of profit or trust in the United States. In other words, he couldn't run for the Senate again. To lessen this punishment, the government allowed Fall to select his own prison, and he wasn't actually locked up until October 7, 1929. The navy collected $43 million from the individuals and companies found guilty in the scandal.

In the meantime other things were happening. In 1925 the Hughes Tool Company developed a new bit, this one twice as efficient as the previous one and began to rent it to oil drillers.

In 1926 the Eastern States Standard Oil Company decided that its name was too long to put on one sign and came out with a new logo—ESSO.

On May 20–21, 1927, a lanky air corps pilot in a single-engined airplane made the first solo crossing of the Atlantic

Ocean. The United States had a new hero, Charles Augustus Lindbergh, whose fame hasn't faded.

On November 10, 1928, the Getty Oil Company was formed in Wilmington, Delaware. Its founder, president, and majority stockholder, John Henry Paul Getty, is today the world's richest man, with an income estimated at half a million dollars a week.

By the end of 1930 motor vehicle registrations in the United States were up to 26,749,853. Although it didn't come into general use for a full generation, on May 14, 1931, the first airplane powered by a turbojet engine made a successful flight. The first all-welded ship was built in 1931. It was a small tanker built by

Thirty-six years after it was first introduced, the DC-3 is still in use around the world. This particular aircraft is used by Gulf Oil Corporation to find new sources of oil. Note the magnetometer flown beneath the aircraft on a cable. The ship itself is a flying laboratory. GULF OIL PHOTO.

the Sun Shipbuilding Company, a subsidiary of Sun Oil Company.

The first woman pilot to fly across the Atlantic Ocean by herself, Amelia Earhart, did so on May 20, 1932. The next month the federal government placed a "temporary" tax of one cent per gallon on gasoline. A year later, the tax was "temporarily" extended for two more years.

Throughout the oil industry, new techniques of production and refining were being introduced almost weekly, and each a small improvement, each new idea was old hat within a year or so. The chemists were trying to find new uses for the petrocarbons coming at an ever-increasing volume from ever deeper holes in the earth. The most significant development was made by DuPont, who in 1934 announced it had made from coal (which is chemically quite similar to other petrocarbons) a synthetic fiber they called polymer 66. The DuPont advertising department quickly changed that name to nylon.

The next year the first 100-octane gasoline was manufactured by Standard Oil at its Baton Rouge, Louisiana, refinery, especially for the Southwest air races at Tulsa. Shortly afterward, the first commercial, gas-fired air-conditioning units were offered for sale.

In 1936 the Douglas Aircraft Corporation rolled out the first production model of the DC-3, a fast (180 mph), 21-passenger airliner, which Douglas claimed would revolutionize the air-transport business. For once, the press agents' grandiose statements were true. With the DC-3 American commercial aviation blossomed beyond anyone's wildest dreams. The DC-3, which is still in daily commercial operation almost 40 years later, made commercial aviation a reality. It also created a demand for high-quality aviation fuel in huge quantities.

War came to Europe, in 1939, and in the last month of 1941, to the United States. It was a war in which oil was the deciding factor, and the oil which drove the Allied armies to victory was almost entirely American.

chapter 13

WHILE TRUCKS AND CARS HAD BEEN USED IN WORLD
War I, it was basically an unmechanized war. The World War I
First Infantry division had at its disposal vehicles whose horsepower added up to 4,000. The same division, known as the
"Big Red One," had vehicles with a total horsepower of 187,-
000 in World War II. (The army hasn't yet computed what
horsepower it had available in Vietnam, where each of its
several hundred helicopters developed 2,250 horsepower.)

World War II was a war of machines, each with an enormous
hunger for fuel. There were huge fleets of tanks, trucks, and
jeeps, each requiring gasoline, lubricating oil, and grease. The
American soldier was the best-fed warrior of all times, and his
food was not only carried to him in oil-fueled ships and railroad
cars and trucks, but refrigerated by oil-generated electricity and
prepared on either gas-fired or gasoline-fired stoves. The electricity for his radios and telephones was generated by oil, and the
TNT in his mines and in bombs and artillery shells had come
originally from an oil refinery.

Between December 1941 and August 1945, the Allies consumed 7 billion barrels of oil, and 6 of the 7 barrels (252 billion
gallons) were American. The war production alone (with the
exception of gasoline, civilian consumption of oil products went
up, not down, during the war) was equal to one-fourth of all the

oil produced in the United States from Colonel Drake's first well until the war started.

The story of aviation fuel, avgas, goes back before the war. Engineers and chemists had since 1925 decided that a "perfect, no-knock" fuel would have an octane rating of 100. The same sort of gasoline that comes out of the high-test pump at any gas station today was available then, but it was a laboratory chemical substance costing about $20.00 a gallon.

By a complex chemical process called polymerization, chemists of the Shell Oil Company produced a substance known as di-isobutylene, which had eight atoms of carbon to sixteen atoms of hydrogen (C_8H_{16}). By a relatively simple process two more atoms of hydrogen could be added to di-isobutylene, turning it into iso-octane (C_8H_{18}).

Shell could make this near-perfect no-knock fuel for about 35 cents a gallon. Since the cost before its development paid off was $20.00 a gallon, Shell felt justified in charging the army air corps 71 cents a gallon for the first carload lot of iso-octane ever manufactured. The air corps had a tank car (18,750 gallons) sent to Wright Field (later Wright Patterson Air Development Center) in Dayton, Ohio, in April 1934.

Shell employed in those days a man who was serving two masters. His name was James Doolittle, and he was a former army air corps pilot. He had left the service to become manager of Shell's aviation department, and he had become a well-known racing pilot. Air races in those days were held close to the ground around pylons, like boat races around markers on the surface of the water. Doolittle's Gee Bee, a low-winged, stubby little airplane that was mostly engine, was as well-known in its day to racing fans as any Indianapolis or NASCAR racing car is known to fans today.

But Doolittle couldn't completely take off his uniform. He thought the United States was headed for war and that a good portion of that war would be fought in the air. He knew that a tremendous advantage would go to the nation whose aircraft would be powered by engines capable of handling 100-octane fuel. At full throttle an engine burning 100-octane fuel was 15–30 percent more powerful than one burning then standard (75-octane) aviation gasoline. At cruising speed, 100-octane gasoline gave much better mileage than standard gas, which to Doolittle meant that if American aircraft engines were burning 100-octane, the fighters and bombers could cruise farther than the enemy and in a tight spot have a 15–30 percent power advantage.

Doolittle's evangelism on behalf of high-octane fuel was greeted suspiciously by the military establishment. If he was so interested in the army air corps, why had he resigned from the service? Wasn't he, after all, an employee of Shell, whose business was selling gasoline? And, if he were a soldier, couldn't he see the wisdom of the policy the military was trying to put into effect of having one fuel for everything with an engine, from a motorcycle to a four-engine bomber?

Doolittle kept repeating his basic facts: 100-octane avgas would give American planes an unquestioned advantage over all others. He had to make the same speech again and again, not only to the army but to Shell, whose executives at first could see little merit in investing vast sums of money to make a fuel nobody wanted.

At Wright Field, the army air corps developed a fuel that was blended of part high-quality California aviation gasoline, part Shell's iso-octane, part tetraethyl lead (3 or 4 cubic centimeters per gallon). The result was 100-octane fuel that cost considerably less than pure iso-octane would have cost.

Standard Oil put its first iso-octane refinery on stream in 1935. It had a capacity of 100 barrels a day. Standard almost immediately started construction of a larger refinery, and Shell, by June of 1936, had built 3 refineries with a total capacity of 6 million gallons of iso-octane a year. During the second half of

1935 the air corps bought 900,000 gallons of 100-octane avgas, 600,000 from Shell and 300,000 from Standard.

Then, in a highly unusual step, the air corps made public the results of its testing of the high-octane fuel, probably because it knew that unless it did, the advocates of one fuel for everything would have their way. Wright Aeronautical Company immediately began building a new aircraft engine with an 8–1 compression ratio, the highest compression ever. And finally, in 1936, the army air corps made it official: all aircraft (except training planes) intended for the air corps after January 1, 1938, must have high-compression engines designed for 100-octane fuel.

Doolittle, having won his fight with the army, now devoted his considerable energy to fighting people who worked for Shell. He wanted production capability increased beyond what anyone else could see any need for. He was aware, too, that there was a follow-the-leader philosophy prevalent in the oil business. If Shell started to increase its iso-octane capability, Standard and the others would do the same thing.

In May 1939, Doolittle found out that the total American production of iso-octane was 5,790 barrels a day. Jersey Standard made 48.3 percent of it, Shell 25.3 percent, and 4 other companies the rest. By November of the same year, daily production was up to almost 12,000 barrels. Shell was now making 40.3 percent of it, Jersey Standard 25.2 percent, and Texaco, which had just begun production, 11.3 percent, with the rest produced by 4 other companies. By October 1940 as the war worsened in Europe, production was up to 20,000 barrels a day. When the Japanese bombed Pearl Harbor, the American oil industry was making 40,000 barrels of iso-octane a day. And almost with relief, Jimmy Doolittle of Shell put his uniform back on and returned to active duty as Maj. James H. Doolittle, U.S. Army Air Corps.

The Japanese bombed Pearl Harbor, our largest navy base,

on Sunday, December 7, 1941. The next day, before the wheels of government could start moving and Congress could officially declare war, the first meeting of the Petroleum Industry War Council was held in Washington.

It was an unusual meeting. Experienced, highly paid executives who had risen to the top in their business at least partially because they had been able to stick corporate knives in the backs of the competition found themselves sitting at a table with the same competitors with the intention of working together. The first thing the military did was ask the important question: could production of aviation gas (avgas) immediately be doubled from 40,000 barrels a day to 80,000?

The military said that plans would have to be made, starting immediately, to raise avgas production eventually to 150,000 barrels a day, 4 times what it was. (The military was wrong; it eventually required 4 times that much avgas, 600,000 barrels—25,200,000 gallons—a day.)

By making small changes in their refining techniques and by changing working hours—in other words, getting the most production out of existing facilities—it would be possible to raise avgas production 6,000 barrels a day (15 percent). But that wasn't going to be enough.

Tetraethyl lead entered the picture, the same lead that was to provide so much concern to environmentalists thirty years later. Lead was already being mixed with gasoline in the refining of avgas because it raised the octane rating so quickly. One cubic centimeter (cc) of lead added to one gallon of "simple gasoline" (the gasoline as it comes from the first refining process) will raise its octane rating from seventy to eighty-one. Three ccs of lead will raise it to eighty-eight. Four ccs will raise the rating to ninety.

Because lead fouls engine parts, particularly spark plugs, the military had established a maximum level of three ccs of lead per gallon of avgas. But now, because it had to have the avgas, it raised the permissible lead content to four ccs per gallon. But even this wasn't going to provide avgas in the quantities needed.

All gasoline is blended, because all crude is different. While the end product of refineries is standardized—avgas with an octane rating of 100/130 is the same quality gas wherever it's pumped into a tank—what goes into it is different at every refinery. Some crude oil is better for the making of fuel than others, while some crude can be most efficiently made into asphalt or lubricating oil. When some crude oil is first refined, the result would include large quantities of low-octane gasoline and very small quantities of high-octane fuel. At another refinery, the first result of refining would be large quantities of asphalt or of heavy lubricating oils and smaller quantities of very high-octane gasoline stock.

Before Pearl Harbor the mixing of the various stocks of petroleum products had been a concern of each individual oil company. The amounts of various types of petroleum the refineries produced were jealously guarded secrets. The secrecy had been a tradition of the oil business since Colonel Drake.

Overnight it was gone. Every company furnished the Petroleum Administration for War (PAW) with a daily report of what kind of feed stock it had produced and how much of it. The PAW issued blending orders, which saw tank cars of Texaco 70-octane feed stock shipped to a Shell refinery for blending with Esso 80-octane, Shell 100-octane, and tetraethyl lead from still another oil company. In turn, each oil company furnished feed stock and received feed stock to achieve the most efficient blending of all fuel.

As production of avgas soared, so did the military requirements for it, and so did the requirement for even higher octane ratings. Avgas, like all gasoline burned in an internal combustion engine, is mixed with a certain proportion of air. Aviation engineers found out that by mixing more avgas with less air they could temporarily increase the power of aircraft engines as much as 30 percent. They couldn't run the engines for long under these conditions, but for a couple of minutes in an aerial dogfight or to get the added power to lift a heavily loaded bomber off a runway, it was something they had to have.

Avgas took on a double rating. Avgas which would under "lean" mixture conditions (cruising) give 100-octane performance but which would under "rich" mixture conditions give 130-octane performance became known as 100/130. Until after the Allied invasion of France in 1944, there was even an avgas with an octane rating of 100/150.

As this frantic effort to produce fuel for the armed forces and our allies got under way, the United States was taking a licking in the Pacific. The Japanese attack on Pearl Harbor had nearly wrecked our fleet. With the fleet gone, there was no way to send supply ships to the Philippine Islands, where troops under Gen. Douglas MacArthur fought a heroic, doomed battle against the Japanese. A Japanese submarine even surfaced off the coast of California and fired a dozen rounds, without much success, at a shore-side oil refinery.

American morale began to sag and then droop. Then suddenly, there was proof that we could fight back. President Roosevelt announced on the radio that a flight of American bombers, which had taken off from "Shangri-La" (an imaginary city in Tibet), had on April 18, 1942, bombed Tokyo and other cities in Japan. The bombers, the president announced, had been under the command of Lt. Col. Jimmy Doolittle.

By the time Doolittle got back to Washington to receive from the president the blue-starred Medal of Honor, the country's highest award for valor, he was Brigadier General Doolittle, and the details of the story came out.

It was well-known that the only aircraft which could be launched from the deck of an aircraft carrier were those aircraft specifically designed for that purpose—single-engine navy fighters and dive bombers and torpedo-launching aircraft. Doo-

*Taking off from "Shangri-La" to bomb the Japanese homeland.
The aircraft carrier was the U.S.S.* Hornet. U.S. AIR FORCE PHOTO.

*Doolittle's aviation exploits before the war had seen him
decorated by many foreign governments, including the Japanese.
He returned his Japanese medal to the Japanese—tied to this
bomb—when he led his B-25s over Tokyo.* U.S AIR FORCE PHOTO.

little, who was almost as persuasive as he was courageous, talked the air force out of a flight of B-25 bombers, twin-engined land airplanes which barely fit on the deck of an aircraft carrier. Then he recruited a force of pilots and aircrewmen for an unspecified dangerous mission. In great secrecy the airmen and planes came together at Eglin Air Force Base on the Florida gulf coast. The dimensions of an aircraft carrier's deck were marked off on a runway deep in the scrub pine of the airbase. The technique was simple. The tail of the aircraft was attached to the ground. The pilot ran his throttles full forward, and when the engines were screaming, the rope was cut with an axe. The plane was shot, like a rock from a sling shot, into the air.

The aircraft were loaded aboard an aircraft carrier and transported near the Japanese coast. Bad luck struck the mission when the carrier and its escorts were spotted by the Japanese. The aircraft carrier, too valuable to be lost, had to run from the Japanese navy. They were still too far off the coast for their planned flight; taking off then meant that some, if not all, of the aircraft would not be able to make their destinations in China after bombing Japan.

Doolittle gathered his men, explained the situation, and said that he was going to bomb Tokyo no matter what the consequences, but he wouldn't order anyone else to go with him. To a man, the others volunteered to go along.

The mission was a success. Tokyo was bombed, and the Japanese thereafter had to divert large forces to protect their home islands, which made a great contribution to our war effort. The Japanese were furious. Some of the crews of the bombers which ran out of gas and landed in Japan were tried as war criminals and beheaded with Samurai swords. Almost all of the planes were lost.

But the boost to the morale of the American people seemed worth the sacrifice. Before the Doolittle raid, the armed forces of the United States had suffered one defeat after another. Doolittle's men proved that we did have the ability to win. But as the war falls into historical perspective, more and more historians are coming to believe that Jimmy Doolittle's most significant contribution to our war effort was not his heroism in leading the B-25s over Tokyo, but his bulldog tenacity before the war began in begging, cajoling, and demanding that the air corps and the oil industry plan their war efforts on the use of billions of gallons of high-octane aviation gasoline that at the time was an expensive laboratory curiosity. Jimmy Doolittle, who had left Shell on military leave as a major, returned after the war to a vice-presidency of the company as Lieutenant General Doolittle.

Even before the war started it was obvious to some people that the transportation of oil—both crude oil and the products of the refineries—was going to pose enormous problems. The first pinch came before the United States was at war. The Germans were well aware that England's ability to fight (quite separate from the will to fight) depended on an unbroken flow of oil to the British Isles, so they did their best to shut off the flow.

Much of the British oil supply came in ships from the Caribbean and the gulf coast of Texas. It took a tanker a month to make the round trip. The Germans sent out their submarine fleet with orders to devote as much time as possible to sinking the British tankers. Technically, the United States was neutral before December 1941, and oil could not be carried in American tankers from American ports to England.

By closing one eye to ethics, however, it was decided that there was nothing wrong in shipping oil for England from Houston to Halifax, Nova Scotia. It was certainly within our rights to transport our own oil in our own ships to our good friends the Nova Scotians. If the German navy didn't like it, they could take on the United States Navy.

What the Nova Scotians did with the oil, we said, was their business. If they wanted to buy the oil and then sell it to the English, that was their business. The result was that the British tankers now traveled only as far as Nova Scotia, rather than to the gulf or the Caribbean for their oil. This cut the length of their trip in half, so it allowed the transportation of twice as much oil in the same ships. And, of course, no oil was sunk between the gulf and Nova Scotia.

Fifty American tankers, previously engaged in hauling oil to New York and New England were diverted to this new market, so a means had to be found to supply New York and New England with the oil previously carried in the fifty tankers.

Railroad tank cars were available, and they were put to use, although it cost ten times as much to ship oil by rail as it did by sea. By running extra trains, carrying extra cars, and running most of them as priority freight, the rail movement of petroleum to the East was increased thirty-fold.

But the oil men realized that this wasn't a solution at all. For one thing, the cost was prohibitive. For another, if the United States (most thinking people thought "*when* the United States") got into the war, the Germans were going to start sinking American tankers as quickly as they were sinking English tankers.

The most efficient way to ship oil overland is by pipeline, and the oil industry, meeting informally, decided that this was the answer. They would build a pipeline or pipelines bigger and longer than any ever built. The first proposal was staggering. They told the government they wanted to build a pipeline 20 inches in diameter and run it from Houston, Texas, to New York City. It would cost an estimated $70 million.

This proposal might have been accepted by the government, had not one oil man spilled the whole story. The twenty-inch pipeline was a stopgap measure; what they really wanted to build—because the nation needed it—was a big pipeline two feet in diameter. When they had that out of the way, they could come up with some other ideas.

The proposal for a twenty-inch pipeline was rejected by the government in September 1941. The government spokesman said that the demands of the country for steel and other products wouldn't permit the allocation of enough material to build a pipe large enough for a man to crawl through from Texas to New York. In February 1942 after we were at war, the government rejected the proposal for the large-diameter line as well, citing the same reasons.

But that didn't end it. On March 23, 1942, nearly a hundred oil men who had spent their careers fighting each other gathered in Tulsa, Oklahoma, to band together to fight bureaucratic blindness. They met in continuous session for three days and three nights, and the telephone lines were tied up as some of the most powerful men in the country explained their position, sometimes forcefully, to members of Congress. The pipelines were needed: without them the war could not be fought.

The result was the formation of the War Emergency Pipe Lines Corporation, a nonprofit organization chartered by the Congress, to build and operate two pipelines. The pipelines were named what the oil men had been calling them all along—the "big inch" and the "little big inch."

The stockholders of War Emergency Pipe Lines, Inc., were Atlantic Refining Company, Cities Service, Gulf, Pan American, Shell, Sinclair, Socony (later called Mobil), Standard of New Jersey, Sun, Texaco, and Tidewater. Never before, anywhere in the world had such a conglomerate been formed. And not only money went into the pot. Executives from the owning companies went to work for War Emergency Pipe Lines, taking small or no salaries at all from it, although they often remained on the payrolls of their own companies. W. Alton Jones, president of Cities Service, became president of War Emergency Pipe Lines. Burt Hall, president of Texaco Pipe Lines, became superintendent of construction. Jersey Standard's W. R. Finney became chief designer. From all over the country huge cartons of aerial photographs of land and crates of plans for pipelines came together at War Emergency's offices to get the big inch and the little big inch going. The material, worth millions of dollars, was furnished free of charge.

By the time permission came to start construction in August 1942, War Emergency Pipe Lines was ready. The first section of big inch pipe was laid in Texas in August. On December 31, 1942, the first oil was fed into the pipe even before the terminus was finished. By the time the first oil had been pumped 1,478 miles, the terminus was in, and thereafter the flow of oil was uninterrupted.

The big inch replaced 75 tankers. It moved as much oil as 30,000 railroad tank cars could move.

The little big inch was started later, with the first section laid in February 1943. It took a year to lay 1,714 miles of 20-inch pipe from Houston to Linden, N.J. By the time the war was over, the two pipelines had delivered 380,000,000 barrels (1,596,000,000 gallons) of oil, more than half of it for purely military purposes.

Another kind of pipeline, one that would have a direct military application, was the brainchild of S. S. "Syd" Smith of Shell, and he saw the need for it long before the military itself did. An oil man to the core, Smith watched the Nazi *blitzkrieg* invasion of Poland and wondered where they got the gas to run all those tanks so far. When he studied the Nazi operation, he saw that his suspicions were correct, that one of the Nazis' major problems had been the supply of fuel for tanks and trucks. Syd Smith realized that the entry of the United States into the war was inevitable and that to win the war, we would have to do anything the Germans could do, only better.

Our tanks would require just as much fuel as the German tanks, and all of it would have to be transported over long distances. The obvious solution was a pipeline, not a huge one, like the big inch, nor a permanent one buried in the ground, but one which could be laid very quickly by relatively unskilled labor and operated by other unskilled labor after installation. What the army needed, Smith decided in 1939, was a portable pipeline which would work like an oversized garden hose. Civilian pipelines pumped oil products from huge tanks at one end to huge pipes at the other end. A military pipeline with the tank farm of a civilian pipeline at both ends was out of the question because a tank farm near the front lines would be an easily recognizable and vulnerable target. The military pipeline would have to end in hoses from which fuel could be pumped directly into GI tank trucks. Nothing that would meet these specifications had ever been thought of or attempted before.

Instead of huge sections of pipe weighing thousands of pounds, Smith's design called for twenty-foot sections of pipe weighing far less. (Ultimately, he got the weight down to ninety pounds). Valves and pumps and the other mechanical parts of a pipeline were built into twenty-foot sections. Instead of being welded together in a continuous length, they would be held together by a circular clamp with a rubber seal fitting around flanged ends. The clamp would be sealed by tightening just one bolt.

Smith worked on his idea for almost two years before anyone paid any attention to him. He solved the problem of eliminating the tank farm at the end of the pipeline by inventing switches for the pumps that worked only when pressure in the pipe dropped. When nothing was flowing out of the pipe's far end, the pumps shut down automatically. They came back on automatically when someone opened the valves at the far end of the line and the pressure dropped. Not only did this eliminate the tank farm, but it did away with the elaborate communications system between pumping stations that the permanent pipeline required.

The only way to get gasoline into China was by truck over the 700-mile Burma Road. But since there were no gasoline stations along the Burma Road, the trucks carrying the gasoline had to carry enough gasoline for the trip from Burma to China and then for the trip back. A truck carrying 320 "jerry" cans of

A camouflaged oil tank in Italy, with the pipeline leading in.
U. S. ARMY PHOTO.

Army engineers lay oil pipeline to the front lines in Italy during World War II. U.S. ARMY PHOTO.

A dockside pumping unit in North Africa, where fuel is unloaded directly from ships to storage tanks on shore. U.S. ARMY PHOTO.

gasoline, each holding 5 gallons, needed 200 cans of the gas for its own fuel, so only 120 cans, 600 gallons, actually got to China for use.

In October 1941 J. H. Hall of the Shell pipeline department was loaned to the government and sent to China to see if Smith's portable pipeline could be used along the Burma Road. When the Japanese attacked Pearl Harbor and stepped up their war effort, getting back home posed great problems, but Hall made it by the middle of February 1942.

Smith, in the meantime, had enough confidence in his idea to order the production of pipe and other material for the line. He wasn't surprised when Hall came back and reported to the army that Smith's pipeline was just what was needed. Two weeks later the Japanese chased the British out of Rangoon (the eastern terminus of the proposed pipeline) and the question became academic.

The pipeline, however, was quickly taken over by the army and sent to North Africa, where 4 different pipelines (ranging in length from 75 to 300 miles) were put to work to support Patton's tanks and to provide fuel to our British allies. As soon as the first pipeline was in and proved its worth, the army placed orders for thousands of miles of pipeline.

After North Africa portable pipelines became a standard item of military equipment. They were used wherever the United States Army took its vehicles, and their use freed the roads of Europe for tactical vehicles. The American version of the *blitzkrieg* made the earlier German action look like slow motion.

Syd Smith (like John Browning, who invented the army's machine gun, automatic rifle, and pistol) had patented equipment and techniques the army had to have whatever the cost. And, like Browning, he turned them over to the government at no charge, as his contribution to the war effort. Smith received for his efforts the Medal of Merit, signed by the president of the United States, for "patriotism of the highest type."

chapter 14

LESS THAN TWENTY-FOUR HOURS AFTER THE JAPA-
nese surrendered unconditionally to General of the Army Douglas
MacArthur aboard the battleship *Missouri* in Tokyo Bay, the
government ended gasoline rationing. Long lines of automobiles
pulled into service stations across the country.

The gasoline they got from a Shell pump was very likely
Texaco gasoline or Esso or some other brand, for the distribution
system couldn't be instantly shifted back to its peacetime operation, but it *was* gasoline, and it was ration-free, and it was a
better gasoline, generally speaking, than what had been available
before the war.

The first cars that came off the assembly lines were really
1942 models with slightly rearranged chrome decorating strips,
but the automotive engineers were already furiously at work
redesigning engines to take advantage of high-octane fuel,
which meant high-compression engines.

There was no postwar slump in the oil business, no readjust-
ment to lower consumption. The reverse was true. The demand
for oil increased with the coming of peace, for automotive and
other uses. At the end of 1945 there were 31 million motor
vehicles in the United States. By 1951 there were 50 million. By
1972, the number passed 100 million. In 1945 there were fewer
than 700 diesel-powered locomotives on American railroads. By

1950 there were 4,400. Today, there are more than 10,000, and the steam locomotive is an interesting relic of a bygone time.

The number of farm tractors doubled and then doubled again, and at the same time the tractor engine grew larger, hungrier for more fuel. With the end of the war came a building boom, not only making up for the housing which was not built during the war, but going far beyond that as the government made guaranteed loans available to veterans. Thus people who otherwise would not have been able to manage a conventional mortgage now could get one through the Veteran's Administration.

Fuel oil for home heating had always been available at a good price, because much of it was a by-product of gasoline refining. During the war the coal miners struck for higher wages, which pushed the price of coal higher on the marketplace. The result was that millions of new homes came equipped with oil-burning, not coal-burning, furnaces, because fuel oil heating was now not only more convenient (no fires to bank, no ashes to haul) but cheaper. So the demand for fuel oil soared.

In 1910 coal had provided 84.8 percent of the energy consumed in America. Water power had provided 3.3 percent, and oil and natural gas together 11.9 percent. By 1950 oil and natural gas were the source of 56.9 percent of the energy the country used, and the percentage continues to climb.

The demand caused two problems. The first was the availability of crude oil from which to make all the things on the large—and growing—list of petroleum products, and the second was the transportation of both crude oil, natural gas, and the products of the refinery.

In the years immediately following the war, the oil companies looked to the ocean or, at least, the submerged continental shelf miles offshore for new supplies of oil at home. They began exploratory drilling and then began production in the far corners of the globe to meet the ever-growing demand.

There had been oil fields in Louisiana almost since Spindle-

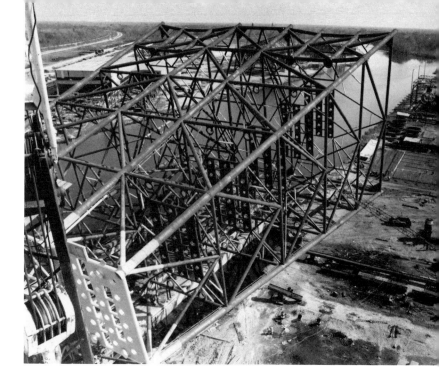

The size of the offshore drilling platforms staggers the mind.
This section of a Humble rig (shown under construction) is
twenty-three stories tall. Notice the construction dragline
at right. HUMBLE OIL PHOTO.

En route to the drilling site, the subsurface portion of the
platform dwarfs the ocean-going tug at right. HUMBLE OIL PHOTO.

The completed platform stands in 210 feet of water where Humble Oil & Refining Company recently tapped a reservoir of natural gas, 100 miles south of Morgan City, Louisiana. HUMBLE OIL PHOTO.

top. In 1955 the largest oil field in Louisiana, pumping 30,000 barrels a day, was miles offshore, under 50 feet of water in the Gulf of Mexico.

Oil was found in vast quantities in Arabia, South America, North Africa, and on the North Slope of Alaska, proving that climate had nothing whatever to do with oil sources. While the problem of finding oil wasn't really solved, there was enough available oil to make the industry turn its attention to getting it from the well head to the refinery and then to the consumer.

It should be noted here that prophets of doom announcing that the supply of oil is about to be exhausted have been around the oil industry from the very beginning. In 1920 the highly respected head of the United States Geological Survey (the man who replaced the man who said they would never find oil at Spindletop) announced officially that domestic oil supplies would be completely exhausted in twenty years. Chemists and others were sent to Scotland then to look into the possibility of extracting oil from shale. Twenty-six years later, in 1946, virtually the same cry that oil was about to be exhausted was made, and again specialists were ordered to look into shale as a possible source of oil. Today, the same cry is being heard.

During July 1973 the United States imported about 8 million barrels of oil a day, a substantial portion of it, perhaps half, from Saudi Arabia. For the sake of argument, assume that Saudi Arabia furnishes all 8 million barrels of crude oil every day. That's less than 3 billion barrels a year. The most pessimistic opinion of Saudi Arabia's proven reserves is 150 billion barrels —50 years worth. Optimistic opinions start at 200 billion barrels and run upward past 600 billion to several trillion. And the key word here is proven reserves. A proven reserve is oil known to be in the ground because a well has been drilled. Geologists and others can make very precise estimates of the size of the pool from a number of pool and geological characteristics. There is little purpose right now in spending millions of dollars exploring for more oil in Saudi Arabia, when there is already (depending on whose opinion you prefer) 50 to 300 years' supply (at present production levels) already discovered.

Proven reserves of oil in the United States are said to be from 40 to 60 billion barrels. Again, the key phrase is proven reserves. Oil companies are reluctant to boast about their proven reserves. It is to their interest to paint a public image of themselves as being close to the brink of financial disaster, with their natural assets nearly expended, as they desperately search for more oil. (Their reaction is understandable, for as long as the oil industry has existed, it has been a splendid target for politicians, originally as a source of revenue, more recently as a "despoiler of nature.")

The 60 billion proven reserve estimate includes the oil known to be under the ground on Alaska's North Slope. Few oil fields have ever produced less than their proven reserves, and exploration of the North Slope (and related fields) nearly came to a stop in the early 1970s when there was a great hue and cry from the conservationists who protested the potential damage to the ecology from the erection of a pipeline to carry crude oil from Alaska to the refineries of the West Coast.

The conservationists delayed the construction of the pipeline for several years. It has been alleged that the oil industry purposefully arranged for a gasoline and fuel oil shortage to remind the American people of their dependency on oil. The oil industry violently denies such allegations and blames the conservationists, who they charge, kept them from building necessary refining and other processing facilities under the guise of protecting the ecology. Therefore, according to the oil industry, insufficient refining capacity rather than a lack of crude oil has been responsible for the shortage.

And the oil companies point out that the antipollution devices with which automobiles must now, by federal law, be equipped have cut gasoline mileage in half, which doubles gasoline de-

Humble Oil's Webster, Texas, pipe farm in 1940. HUMBLE OIL PHOTO.

mand. The battle seems destined to go on for some time.

While it is true that oil, like any other natural resource, is not inexhaustible, it is also true that the oil business so far, and for the foreseeable future, is capable of meeting the demand. To do so may require doing things that have never been done before, but doing things that have never been done before is the way the oil business has operated since Oil Creek.

While they were being planned and built, there had been serious concern with the postwar future of the big inch and the little big inch. With the end of the war, would they still be needed? Would the demand for that much oil be there? What about the tankers? Would they be rendered useless by the pipelines or the other way around?

The demand was there. The demand for natural gas, in fact, was so great that in December 1946 both the big inch and the little big inch were turned over to gas transmission. The first Texas natural gas pumped through the big inch arrived in Ohio on December 11, 1946, and it has been flowing ever since.

The two wartime pipelines not only proved their worth but provided a wealth of information about pipeline operation. The larger the pipeline, the more cheaply it could transport oil. A 20-inch diameter pipeline, for example, required twice as much steel as a 10-inch line. But it would carry 4 times as much oil with less effort. Because there was less friction against the side of the pipe in the larger line, fewer pumping stations (proportionately) were required. In terms of cost, a fully loaded 20-inch line could transport oil for 45 percent of the cost of pumping it through a fully loaded 10-inch line.

One of the first postwar lines built was a joint venture of Cities Service, Sinclair, Shell, and the Texas Pipeline Company. A 20-inch pipe was laid from Jal, New Mexico, to transport Permian Basin crude to Midland, Texas. From Midland, where more Permian Basin oil was added, to Wichita Falls, Texas, the line was 22 inches in diameter, and from Wichita Falls to Cushing, Oklahoma, the pipe laid was 24 inches in diameter. The line is capable of carrying 385,000 barrels of oil daily.

Another line of twenty-two-inch pipe was built by the Texas Pipeline Company and Shell north from Cushing to the Shell Wood River refinery, and when that was nearly completed, Shell started laying a new twenty-two-inch line into Missouri. This line crossed five rivers, including the Mississippi. The pipe for it occupied the full-time production of the Youngstown (Ohio) Sheet and Tube Company for eighty-one days, with the mill working twenty-four hours a day, seven days a week. Every thirty-six hours for that period, a sixty-car train left the mill loaded with nothing but pipe.

Most of the postwar pipelines were joint ventures. After a generation of fighting among themselves, the oil companies' cooperation for the World War II war effort convinced everybody that cooperation was not only possible but sometimes profitable as well.

Pipelines soon crisscrossed the country as the railroads had a century before. The difference was that they were practically invisible, even during construction. Highly skilled workers operating complicated, expensive, efficient equipment proved their ability to lay pipe at high speeds and to do it so that often the only indication that a pipeline was under the ground was a small sign telling people not to dig holes. Pumping stations were located either in the terminal points, where they went unnoticed, or in little buildings that looked like somebody's country home.

Exploration for oil deposits meanwhile was going on around the world, and transporting that oil or the refinery products of it to the consumer could not be handled entirely by pipeline nor by standard-sized tankers.

Pipelines carried oil across mountains and jungles and deserts to seacoasts, where it was pumped aboard ever-larger tankers for transport by sea to the consumer. One enterprising Greek looked even further into the future than most oil men and went

Oil goes up and down the Mississippi, too. Here the Mobil Leader *out of Beaumont for Chicago pushes a barge train past St. Louis's Gateway Arch and some beached old sternwheelers.*
MOBIL OIL PHOTO.

into the oil transport business, starting out with surplus tankers he purchased at a fraction of their cost from the American War Assets Administration. Shipping oil in them made Aristotle Onassis one of the world's richest men.

By the end of the 1950s the insatiable hunger for oil saw supertankers put into service. These were—and are—enormous vessels, far larger than anything used through the end of World War II, with deadweight tonnage running as high as 75,000 tons. They were soon followed by supersupertankers, weighing from 80,000 to 100,000 tons. And even this wasn't sufficient capacity to keep the refineries running. Next came monster tankers weighing from 200,000 to 250,00 tons. (It was one of these, the *Torrey Canyon*, carrying 119,000 tons of Kuwait crude oil, which went aground on the southwest coast of England and caused concern about oil pollution of the world's oceans and beaches.)

Then Gulf Oil, which had a large European market for refinery products and large supplies of crude oil available in Kuwait, decided it had to have larger ships, even though the ships could not pass through the Suez Canal (which was then in operation) and would have to go from a specially built loading port in the Gulf of Kuwait around the Cape of Good Hope to a specially built off-loading port at Bantry Bay in Southwest Ireland. It was becoming more and more difficult to find words to describe the size of tankers. The standard tanker through World War II had a deadweight of 16,500 tons. The postwar tankers with deadweights up to 75,000 tons were naturally called "supertankers." If "supersupertanker" described vessels with a deadweight of 100,000 tons, what could you call a tanker weighing 200,000 tons, and, for Gulf's purposes, what could you call a tanker which was to weigh 326,000 deadweight tons? The problem was solved simply. The largest vessels ever floated were called Bantry class tankers.

The huge liner *Queen Elizabeth* is 1,032 feet long, about one-

Mobil Oil Corporation's supersupersupertanker, the Mobil Progress, *underway.* MOBIL OIL PHOTO.

An aerial view of a barge dock where American gasoline is being delivered to Germany. U.S. ARMY PHOTO.

fifth of a mile. The Bantry class tankers are 103 feet longer—1,135 feet. That's 150 feet longer than the Eiffel Tower is tall.

From the bottom of the hull to the upper deck, Bantry class tankers measure 110 feet, the height of a 10-story building. Sixty-two tennis courts could be fitted on the 175,400 square feet of the main deck. There are 22 tanks, holding a total of 2,250,000 barrels of oil. That's enough to fill the tanks of 10 million family automobiles. Two engines, each developing 17,000-shaft horse-power, move this enormous vessel through the seas at 16 knots.

The ships were built in Japan by Ishikawajima-Harima Heavy Industries at Yokohama and by Mitsubishi Heavy Industries at Nagasaki. They were too much even for the largest, most modern shipyards in the world. When the *Universe Ireland*, the first built, was launched she was minus her bow section and a major portion of her port side. She was just too big for the building dock.

The *Universe Ireland* was finished in the bay and then taken outside the bay, where her tanks were filled with sea water. Once that happened, she could not return to Tokyo Bay or any other bay in the world except Bantry Bay, half-way around the world. Even in Kuwait she was so deep that the oil-loading facilities had to be located ten miles off the Kuwait coast.

The offshore terminal at Kuwait was the first of its kind any-where in the world. A huge bargelike vessel was built in Greece and then towed to Kuwait. Enormous legs were lowered through ninety-five feet of water and then forced seventy feet into the bed of the sea. The barge was hoisted out of the water, and then it was connected by a pipeline to the shore. The pipeline diam-eter was forty-eight inches, making it the largest pipeline (as well as the largest submarine pipeline) in the world. Loaded with oil, 2,250,000 barrels of it, the *Universe Ireland* set out for Bantry Bay, 11,000 miles away, a month's voyage.

No one had ever before handled a ship of this size. The com-pany (National Bulk Carriers, Inc.) which built and owns the

vessels and then leases them to Gulf, had built a miniature Bantry Bay in Holland, complete to model tanker, to give potential
Bantry Bay class tanker captains a month of practice on miniature ships. The miniature ships were large enough to carry an
instructor captain, a trainee captain, and a crew to run the engines. The school and its equipment cost several million dollars.

The trip from Japan to Kuwait and from Kuwait to Ireland
had shown that the ships were stable. Waves which would have
caused a smaller ship to pitch and roll dangerously just bounced
off the sides of the *Universe Ireland* as if she were a breakwater,
with the waves shooting straight up in the air.

But another problem is maneuvering something that large and
that heavy into a pier. Newton's Third Law of Motion, says that
a body in motion tends to stay in motion. All the computations
had been made by computers, of course, so there was no official
worrying. But there was a good deal of unofficial worrying.
Would it be possible to stop 326,000 tons of steel and crude oil
where they wanted it to stop?

By the time the *Universe Ireland* was two miles from Whiddy
Island in Bantry Bay, she had cut her speed to three knots. A
fleet of powerful tugs came out to meet her, like ants trying to
move an oak tree. She was slowed even more, brought abreast of
the jetty, and then moved in sideways at a precise speed of four
inches a second (twenty feet a minute) until she gently nudged
the dock.

The largest vessel ever built had just connected with the largest single stores of energy ever built. The Whiddy Island Terminal, built expressly to handle the Kuwait crude delivered by the
Bantry class tankers, has a capacity of 1 million tons of crude,
stored in 12 tanks, each with a capacity of 600,000 barrels. In
the course of a year, more than 80 million barrels of crude
arrive at Bantry Bay, are unloaded, and are reloaded on smaller
tankers. The pumping system can handle 100,000 barrels
(4,200,000 gallons) an hour.

The Universe Ireland *being nudged into her pier at Bantry Bay.*
GULF OIL PHOTO.

The unloading jetty at Whiddy Island is 1,200 feet offshore. A Bantry class tanker docks at one side of the jetty, and as many as three shuttle tankers dock on the other side of it. They carry crude oil and refinery products from the tanks and refinery to where they are needed throughout Europe.

One of the problems caused by the enormous size of the Bantry class tankers is that they expose enormous surfaces to the wind. If one of the 326,000-ton monsters were allowed to pump her tanks dry and rise out of the water as her weight decreased, the force of slightly more than a gentle breeze would be enough to send her sailing right through the jettys at either Kuwait or Banty Bay. At sea the force of the wind would send her far off course if she were permitted to sail in any condition but low in the water.

The smaller shuttle tankers have a similar problem, although not quite as severe. Both categories of ships require ballast, and the most convenient ballast they can use is water. But water pumped into a tank which previously held crude oil is contaminated with that crude, and if, when an empty tank is needed to carry oil again, the contaminated water is simply pumped over the side, the water would contaminate the sea for hundreds of miles. An elaborate ballast system, both onshore and aboard the ships was constructed, including storage-tank facilities for one million barrels of dirty ballast.

When a shuttle tanker arrives at Bantry Bay, if its arrival coincides with the arrival of a Bantry class giant (the latter are getting to be known as 326s, a reference to their tonnage), it simply pumps its dirty ballast into the tanks of the giant.

If no huge tanker happens to be in port, it pumps the dirty ballast into the dirty ballast storage tanks. When a 326 arrives in port, it simultaneously takes on dirty ballast as it pumps its load of crude ashore.

The giants present so much surface to the wind that sailing becomes a problem. The farther they are out of the water, the

The Universe Portugal, *a Bantry class tanker with her tanks pumped partially dry, rises far out of the water for painting and maintenance.* GULF OIL PHOTO.

The Universe Iran *underway on the high seas, riding low in the water.* GULF OIL PHOTO.

THE LOAD ON TOP SYSTEM

Figure 1

ARRIVING AT DISCHARGE PORT
Full cargo—Clean ballast tank empty.

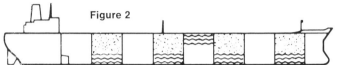

Figure 2

AFTER DISCHARGING CARGO VESSEL PROCEEDS TO SEA
Clean ballast tank full (clean water)—Cargo tanks partially full dirty ballast.

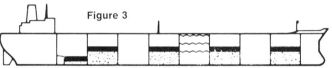

Figure 3

AFTER SEVERAL DAYS AT SEA
Oil settles on top-clean water pumped from bottom Tank cleaning of empty tanks. Tank wash water collected in #8 Tank (waste tank).

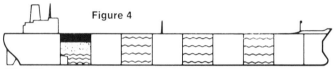

Figure 4

AT SEA
Clean ballast for docking. #8Tank contains waste and all residues for separation.

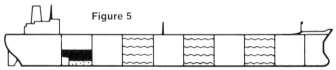

Figure 5

ARRIVING AT LOADING PORT
Clean ballast for docking—Waste tank (#8) drained of all clean water leaving only collected residue. Before loading all clean water pumped into sea.

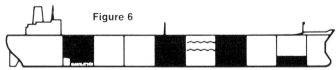

Figure 6

DURING LOADING CARGO
#8 Tank loaded on top of residues.

 **Clean Sea Water**

 **Oil Contaminated Sea Water**

 Crude Oil

larger a surface they present to the winds. Consequently, a good deal of effort goes into making sure that they never draw less than forty feet of water while unloading.

If there is enough ballast in the dirty ballast tanks ashore, fine. If not, water is taken aboard from the bay itself. When all the oil has been pumped ashore and the 326s are away from the jetty and bound for Kuwait and a fresh load, they need only thirty feet of draft, which means getting rid of that much dirty ballast.

But again, the dirty ballast can't be pumped over the side because of the contamination it would cause. Installed on board is a Butterworth Oil Water Separator.* The dirty ballast is pumped through the separator. The oil removed is pumped into a regular oil tank, and the water, now clean, is pumped over the side.

As the tanks are emptied of dirty ballast, they are cleaned by a cleaning system installed as part of the tank. The result of all this is that a Bantry class tanker which left Bentry Bay with most of her tanks filled with dirty ballast arrives at the loading jetty in Kuwait with clean ballast in all the tanks except those which hold the oil reclaimed from the dirty ballast.

As she approaches Kuwait, her suction pumps start up again, filling her tanks with sea water so that she drops lower into the water and reaches the jetty drawing 40 feet of water. This clean ballast is pumped out as the oil from the shore is pumped into her tanks. Eventually, she's low in the water with nothing in her tanks but 94,500,000 gallons of crude oil. Then she sets out for Bantry Bay, and the process starts all over again. Six of these monsters are engaged in this operation right now, and more are in the shipyards.

* No relation to the author, unfortunately.

The load-on-top system. GULF OIL DRAWING.

chapter 15

IN CONSIDERING THE STATISTICS OF OIL CONSUMP-
tion and the fascinating means of getting oil from the well head
through the refinery to the ultimate consumer, the oil well itself
tends to be put in the shadow. But finding oil and drilling for it
are still the most important parts of the oil industry.

It is no longer possible, as it was at Oil Creek, Pennsylvania,
and at Spindletop to find oil or gas bubbling naturally to the
surface of the earth. Those deposits have all been exhausted, and
people now have to drill more deeply (to depths of several
miles) to find oil and gas and then only after geologists have
made extensive surveys to find those characteristics in the crust
of the earth which suggest the possibility that oil may be found.

Finding a potential oil field combines art and science. The
science is geology, the study of the strata of the earth's crust. By
a number of methods, primarily the seismic, geologists are able
to prepare charts showing what strata of rock and shale and salt
and water and sand are under the earth at a specific location.

The basic method of doing this is with explosives. A hole
about seventy-five feet deep is drilled into the earth. Instruments
called geophones (like microphones) are laid out at precise dis-

tances from the hole. An explosive, generally dynamite, is set off in the bottom of the hole. The geophones pick up the sound (actually the shock waves) of the explosion. Geologists can then determine by the time (in small fractions of a second) it takes the shock waves to reach the geophones, what rock strata or sand or salt water is probably under the surface of the earth.

Once a chart has been prepared (and charts are prepared by the thousands) the art comes in. A geologist who can read a chart and judge from it where an oil well should be put down with any high degree of success (say one successful well out of ten in an unproven field) is one of the most valuable employees in the oil industry and is paid accordingly. Seismographical charts of possible oil fields and the opinions of the geologists who have read them are probably the most closely guarded of all industrial secrets.

Exploration, which is fantastically expensive, goes on all the time, with new techniques constantly being introduced. But before any exploration can go on, the oil company must either have obtained the permission of the landowner to conduct the exploration or have leased the mineral rights to the land.

It's that inexact. An oil company will decide, for example, that possibly there is some oil around Mobile Bay, which opens onto the Gulf of Mexico in Alabama. There is general reason to believe there should be. There is oil in Louisiana, not far away, and there is oil fifty miles away in the Citronelle field, and there is oil out in the Gulf of Mexico itself, a hundred miles or so away. And at other places in the world where there are combinations of geological characteristics similar to that found around Mobile Bay oil has been found.

A decision is made to make exploratory studies. Permission of the state, which not only owns the land under water of the bay but which rigidly controls everything to do with oil production within its boundaries, must be sought and obtained to conduct any kind of survey. (In recent years applying for permission to

conduct a preliminary survey has been enough to bring out conservationists and environmentalists, some of whom are com-
mendably interested in making sure that exploration won't hurt
the environment, and some of whom are opposed to anything
connected with exploration.) Since no lasting harm will be done
by conducting preliminary exploration surveys, state governments generally grant this permission readily.

Crews of landmen are sent out. Equipped with precise land
maps, they get permission from private owners of land to conduct either preliminary or seismic surveys of their land and often
must pay for the privilege, even though rights to oil, if any, are
not involved.

Most of these landmen go to great lengths to hide their association with the major oil company which employs them. The
landmen from the Super Mammoth World Wide Oil Company,
for example, might seek permission to conduct a survey as members of the Joe Jones & Son Geology Company and flatly deny
any knowledge that Joe Jones & Son is a wholly owned subsidiary of Super Mammoth. Sometimes the deception works, and
sometimes it doesn't, but, eventually, the landmen obtain permission to survey seismically all the land the company is interested in.

By now, however, it has come to the attention of Great World
Wide & Western Petroleum that Super Mammoth is nosing
around Mobile Bay. Soon there are landmen from the Smith
Brothers Geological Survey knocking at doors and seeking per-
mission to conduct a survey, their association with Great World
Wide a dark secret.

And if the potential of the field (measured by the activity of
the landmen and the geologists) seems large enough, they are
often followed by a half a dozen other landmen and seismic
crews from the other major companies and some smaller ones.

Finally, based on its geologists' opinion of the seismic charts,
each company decides whether the further, far greater expense

of actually drilling for oil should be entailed. (In addition to highly paid company geologists, oil companies commonly consult consulting geologists for an opinion. Most consulting geologists are former company geologists with a good track record for finding oil deposits, who have gone into business selling their opinions to the highest bidder.)

The landmen go out again, this time to acquire mineral rights. Rights to drill for oil on state and federal land are most often auctioned off to the highest builder at the world's most expensive auctions. (When the state of Alaska held the auction for the North Slope fields, it sent the oil companies' checks by chartered jet to New York. So much money was paid that the daily interest on the money was said to be over $125,000. By chartering a jet for $5,000 and rushing the checks to the banks for deposit, the state made another $120,000 in interest.) Private landowners are offered so much money per acre, plus a royalty (generally one-eighth) of all oil recovered. If no oil is found, there is no royalty, of course, but the landowner keeps whatever he is paid for permitting drilling.

As a general rule, one oil well can extract all the oil under a forty-acre piece of ground, and for that reason most states forbid drilling more than one oil well per forty acres. So the landmen have to put together a drilling unit of forty acres. If one person owns all forty of the acres around the site of the intended hole, fine. But that person owns only half of the drilling unit the landmen must lease the mineral rights to the other half from whomever owns it.

No matter where the hole is drilled on a drilling unit, royalties are paid to everybody who owns part of the unit in proportion to the size of their holding. For example, if a drilling unit's 40 acres were split between 3 owners, one person owning 5 acres, another 15, and the third 20, the division of royalties between them, no matter who owned the land where the well was actually drilled, would be 12.5 percent, 37.5 percent, and 50 percent.

Drilling units can be square or long and thin or even jagged. They have to meet the approval of the state, which frowns on odd-shaped units, but the basic consideration is the simple one: 1 well per 40 acres.

Now the oil company must seek permission from the state to drill an oil well. At one time this was a routine no more complicated than getting a building permit and paying a fee. In recent years because of concern with ecology and pollution, it has become far more complicated, and licenses are not granted until the state is sure that the damage (and there is always some damage, if only temporary) to the environment in terms of water and air and noise pollution is both minimal and reasonable. The license commissioner is generally an unhappy soul who agrees with the environmentalists that oil wells are messy and with the drillers that the country needs oil and tries to find a balance between the two opposing sides.

Drilling is done either by the companies themselves or by independent drilling companies, which drill the hole for so much money a foot or so much a day or, sometimes, for part cash and a part interest in the well. Some drilling machinery is enormous beyond description, but it is always designed to be moved once the hole is finished. What it does, however, isn't much—if at all—different from the first oil rigs at Oil Creek. Most drilling is now done with rotary rigs, but some cable rigs are still in use in small fields where great depth is not required.

A cable rig drills its hole by slamming its bit again and again into the ground, battering its way through earth and rock. A rotary rig drills by turning a bit against the dirt and rock. (The fortune of Howard Hughes, one of the richest men in the world, was founded on the Hughes Tool Company, which patented a rotary bit vastly superior to anything in use and then leased it, rather than sold it, to oil drillers.)

When all the preparations have been completed—the surveys are in and evaluated; the landmen have all the land under lease;

the governments' licensing requirements have all been met—the time has come to put down the hole.

First to arrive on the scene is a small utility vehicle of some sort, a jeep or a pickup or a four-wheel drive carry-all, carrying two or three men. All dressed in work clothes, they are probably the highest paid blue-collar workers in the world—the geologist and the tool pusher. The company drilling superintendent or for an independent drilling contractor, the boss himself might be along, but the tool pusher is in charge.

His title dates back to the time of the first oil wells in Pennsylvania, when the tool pusher was the man who pushed the tool into the ground. He is now, without exception, an experienced oilfield expert, combining a knowledge of mechanics, hydraulics, mechanical and electrical engineering, and human psychology. A good tool pusher earns as much as $60,000 a year. It is entirely possible, even probable, that he started his career as an unskilled laborer or roustabout and worked his way up.

The responsibility for the drilling rig from the moment the order is given to put down the hole until the rig is removed is entirely his, and a rig often costs several million dollars. The tool pusher stands there, one eye on the charts and another on the field, and makes the first decisions: that little hill will have to be flattened; the mud tank will have to be scraped out there, and here is where we'll put in the road. A suggestion might be offered or even solicited, but the decisions of the tool pusher are never overridden.

Next a convoy of huge trucks, their tractors and trailers designed and built solely for the oil trade, arrives. A large-sized bulldozer rolls off one of them and begins to scrape a road across the field to the stake in the ground where the hole will go down. As soon as the road is in, the bulldozer starts to scrape out the mud reservoir. Meanwhile, the rig itself, starting with huge diesel engines to provide mechanical and electrical power, starts to go up. (Some newer rigs are "all electric," which means electric motors powered by the diesel engine generators provide mechanical force. Other rigs take mechanical power directly from the diesel engines).

The tower goes up with startling rapidity. The rotary platform
is installed. Drill pipe, in forty-foot lengths, is manhandled from
huge trailer trucks and snaked up inside the derrick tower with a
winch.

The mudman appears on the scene, consults with the geologist
and the toolpusher, and determines the chemical consistency of
the mud which will be forced down the drill pipe, out of the pipe
at the bottom of the hole, and allowed to flow upward, carrying
with it the dirt and chewed-up rock. (The bit is wider than the
drill stem to provide room for the mud to flow back out of the
hole.)

Finally, everything is in place, assembled, and tested. There is
a roar from the diesels, and the rotary table begins to turn. The
bit at the end of the first length of drilling pipe starts chewing
into the ground, moving quickly through the soft dirt. The
pumps are already flooding the hole with mud to carry the dirt
away.

The man in charge of each crew (there are three crews, operating in eight-hour shifts around the clock, seven days a week) is
the driller, sometimes known as the "tour boss," and the word is
most often pronounced "tower." There is one driller, or tour
boss, to each crew. He is responsible only to the tool pusher, and
he aspires to be a tool pusher himself. He has to know everybody
else's job and most frequently has done everybody else's job as
he worked his way up. He controls the machinery, the pressure
applied to the bit, the speed it turns, selects the proper bit itself,
and supervises the others.

High on top of the derrick is his number two man, the derrick
man, who works on a small platform (the monkey bar) whenever
pipe is either being let down into the hole or pulled out (for
example, when it is necessary to replace a worn-out drilling bit).

The derrick man will come down from his perch when the hole is being drilled ("when the string is turning") to supervise the flow of mud into the hole.

Working on the platform itself is the man we see most often in movies about oil-well drilling, the rotary helper. He guides lengths of pipe hanging from the derrick onto the end of the pipe in the rotary platform and screws them together (or unscrews them when the "string is pulled" either to change the bit or for other reasons).

Just off the rotary platform is the engineman, who controls (and maintains) the diesel engines and works the block and tackle used to pull and lower the string of drilling pipe. The rotary helper is commonly called a "roughneck," and it is a term of prestige in the oil fields, a promotion up from the roustabouts who are, comparatively, unskilled laborers who do all the odd jobs around a well and are often not considered quite as members of the drilling crew, but as apprentices aspiring to be roughnecks.

Anywhere from fifteen to twenty-five workers make up the work crew of a rig, working in three shifts of five to eight men each. It's hard, rough, and often dangerous work, but the pay is good and drilling rig workers seem convinced that they are members of an elite group.

The only difference between oil-well drilling onshore and offshore is that the tours are different. Offshore workers work twelve-hour shifts for a week and then have a week off, during which they are transported (generally by helicopter) back to the land.

chapter 16

WHERE OIL EXPLORATION AND EXPLOITATION LIES now is somewhere between the demand of our society for ever more energy and the justifiable outrage of conservationists and environmentalists who protest that finding oil and producing it are destroying the quality of our life. The oil industry, on the one hand, has made ludicrous announcements to the effect that the oil industry is not much dirtier than watchmaking, and the conservationists and environmentalists, on the other hand, have made equally ludicrous announcements that Armaggedon is here, floating on a tide of oil. The truth is somewhere near the middle of the opposing positions. We have had major spills. Offshore drilling rigs in California and elsewhere have broken or ruptured or burned or otherwise failed, pouring vast quantities of crude oil into the oceans. And it has caused great damage.

The oil industry hasn't been entirely blameless. The federal government caught half a dozen major producers in the Gulf of Mexico who had not installed the safety devices required by law. It's not much of a secret that some ocean-going tankers do pump dirty ballast over the side the minute they can't see the coast guard and the coast guard can't see them. Construction of a huge pipeline to carry crude from the North Slope of Alaska was delayed by conservationists and others who convinced the courts that the oil industry's assurances that the pipeline will be fool-proof don't hold water. The demand for oil finally saw Congress rejecting the conservationist-environmentalist arguments.

And when the *Torrey Canyon* went aground and broke up, there was the fear among some people that the Bantry class ships would have the same kind of trouble. This is not to suggest that there won't be other tankers who spill their contents into the oceans of the world. There will be other spills and probably larger ones than the *Torrey Canyon*. By the same token, it is only a matter of time until one of the jumbo jets gets into trouble, and we will have a new record for the most people killed at one time in an aircrash. That will be horrible, of course, and what will be forgotten when that happens is how many millions of people have traveled billions of high-speed miles in great comfort and complete safety. Even when that happens no one will suggest that the jumbo jets be scrapped and people go back to the old way of crossing the ocean in a ship. And if there are to be jumbo jets or, for that matter, any kind of aircraft or any-

A huge Mobil tank truck, towing a tank trailer, fuels a 747 jumbo jet in Hamburg, Germany. MOBIL OIL PHOTO BY JAMES A. FOOTE.

The largest customer for aviation fuel is the U.S. Air Force's C-5A.
In this photo the aerial monster is shown taking on 150,000
gallons of fuel from a KC-135 flying tanker. Two tankers are
required to fill her up. Her tanks hold 318,500 pounds of fuel,
about 49,000 gallons. U.S. AIR FORCE PHOTO.

thing requiring a steady supply of petroleum, there are going to
have to be tankers carrying oil by sea. The JP-4 fuel carried in
the tanks of a jumbo jet leaving Orly Field in Paris for New
York arrives in Europe in the tanks of a Bantry class tanker.

What really happened in the *Torrey Canyon* disaster? March
18, 1967, was a Saturday. The *Torrey Canyon* had left Kuwait
for Milford Haven, England, with 119,000 tons of crude oil for
England's automobiles, aircraft, heating furnaces, and other petroleum needs. She was running on automatic pilot on a true
course of 018 degrees, making 16 knots in a mild sea, with
waves 4 to 5 feet high. She was running low in the water, and the
waves didn't bother her at all.

Her captain had been told that he had to make port that night
on the high tide which would occur at 11:00 P.M. If he missed
that high tide, he would have to wait six days before he could

take his ship into port. He couldn't get in if his draft exceeded fifty-two feet two inches. He was drawing more draft than that right then. He also had a sag in the *Torrey Canyon* hull, amidships, of nine inches. Before he made port, he would have to shift oil from the center tanks to forward and rear tanks and straighten out the hull.

It is not at all uncommon for a ship of that size to be nose heavy or tail heavy or to sag in the middle. The captains of these ocean-going fuel dumps are paid very well, and they are highly intelligent men, of wisdom, responsibility, long experience, and extensive training. He anticipated no problems in bringing his ship safely into port.

On the other hand, he didn't lie abed and let someone else worry about it. He got up early that morning, had breakfast, and went to the bridge to see his chief officer, who had the watch. He gave the chief officer his orders. The *Torrey Canyon* was to swing six miles to the west of the Scilly Isles and then, past them, to swing to the east again for the run across the Bristol Channel into Milford Haven. Then he left the bridge and went to his office.

At half past six in the morning the *Torrey Canyon*'s radar—the best that money could buy—picked up the Scilly Isles. They were twenty-four miles dead ahead, an hour and twenty minutes away at their speed. But the radar showed them to be to the west of the ship, not to the east, where they should have been. The *Torrey Canyon* was apparently about eight miles off course.

Chief officers aboard ships like the *Torrey Canyon* are experienced master mariners, fully licensed to command the ships themselves. The *Torrey Canyon*'s chief officer, when he saw where they were, ordered the helm put over to carry them to the west of the Scillies as he had been ordered to do. Then, as part of the routine, he telephoned the captain and told him what he had done.

The captain at that point exercised his command. He wanted

to arrive at Milford Haven in plenty of time not only to catch the tide, but to shift the cargo when the ship was either stopped completely or just making headway through the sea.

"Put her back on 018 true," the captain ordered. "We'll take her inside the Scillies."

"Yes, sir," the chief officer replied and gave the necessary orders to the helmsman. It wasn't a case of having made a decision and having it challenged and overridden. He had instead followed his original orders, which the captain, exercising his duty, had changed in the interests of the ship and her owners.

Nor was it a case of the captain's accepting a risk in order to get where he wanted to go when he wanted to be there. The Scilly Isles were now twenty-three or so miles to the northwest. To the northeast of the Scilly Isles was the Seven Stones Reef. A perfectly safe channel, six and one-half miles wide, separates the Stones from the Scillies. Anchored north and east of the Stones was Her Majesty's light vessel *Seven Stones*. It was already on the radar. It could be passed on the left (to the west) or to the right. Between H.M.S. *Seven Stones* and the Longships light-house marking Land's End, was a perfectly safe channel eleven and a half miles wide.

By eight o'clock, the captain was on the bridge and in command. The third officer had the watch and was now functioning as navigator. At 8:12 A.M. he told the Captain they were 4.5 miles off the Scillies to the east. Ahead of them, they could see two French lobster boats.

Four minutes later, at 8:18, the captain ordered a slight course change, which would turn the *Torrey Canyon* to the left so that it would pass right down the middle of the 6.5-mile wide channel between the Scillies and H.M.S. *Seven Stones*.

At 8:30 the captain ordered another course change, this time to the right (east) because he became aware that the ship had sailed through some fisherman's nets, and cut them. (Fishermen put their nets down in a channel like this at their own risk. That's where the fish are, but ocean-going ships are not required to change their courses to accommodate fishermen. The captain was simply being courteous.)

At 8:40 the third officer reported their new position, 2.8 miles from the nearest of the stones of the Seven Stones. The captain ordered a new course pointing directly at the Stones. He planned very soon to change course again, and there was plenty of room and time to do this. What he was doing then was avoiding a fishing boat directly ahead of him. Once past that, he planned to swing hard left and finally enter the channel.

A mile off the nearest rock, he gave the order, "Bring her hard to port."

"Hard a port it is, sir," the helmsman echoed, and he swung the massive wheel as far to the left as it would go. The captain left the window and went to the chart table.

"Captain," the helmsman said, "the ship is not turning."

The captain left his charts and first checked the three fuses which controlled the steering mechanism from the wheel. They were all in order on the bridge.

He thought the trouble might lie in the steering motors far below and picked up the ship's telephone to call the engine room. He got the officer's mess by mistake. He hung up and started to dial again. Then he saw what the trouble was.

There was a switch by the steering wheel. It disconnected the wheel when the ship was on autopilot or when the emergency steering mechanism, a lever, was in use. The switch was in the "control" or emergency position. How it got there, no one knows.

The captain ran to the switch, threw it to "manual" and himself turned the wheel. It was then 8:49.

At 8:50 the *Torrey Canyon*, carrying 119,000 tons of crude oil and making 16 knots through moderate seas ran aground onto Pollard Rock of the Seven Stones.

She went aground three-quarters of her length; 14 of her 18

tanks were ruptured, and crude oil started flowing into the sea. As fast as it could surge through holes in the sides of the vessel, 30,000 tons of crude entered the sea. During the next week, another 20,000 tons of crude leaked out more slowly.

Rescue efforts began immediately, of course, and for a few days there was hope that the *Torrey Canyon* could be refloated. On Sunday, March 26, 6 days after she went aground, while salvage vessels were attempting to pull her free, she broke her back and then broke into 3 pieces. Another 50,000 tons of crude poured into the sea. A little less than 20,000 tons of crude remained.

The Royal Air Force and the Royal Navy Air Wing appeared over her. She was bombed with napalm and strafed with rockets. The use of napalm (which is gasoline jellied with naptha) in the Vietnam War made it a dirty word in international politics. The world was shocked to learn that Great Britain not only had napalm ready at hand, but was apparently quite experienced in its use.

Newspapers around the world reported that a "sea of oil 6 inches thick" was headed for English and French beaches. Much oil was indeed headed for the beaches, but the 6-inch thickness was inaccurate. Oil slicks rarely exceed ¼ inch in thickness, and as soon as a slick has time to spread (and it spreads rapidly), the thickness is almost always less than .04 inch.

Excitement approaching hysteria began, both with those in-volved and to people thousands of miles away who were not. The British and French authorities, in particular the British Royal Navy, had contingency plans for oil spills. The trouble with the planning was that no one had ever anticipated an oil spill of this magnitude.

Most of the planning was based on the use of detergents, more properly emulsifiers. The detergents planned for use were a pe-troleum solvent and a so-called surface-acting agent. The idea was that the solvent would thin the crude oil, and then the surface-acting agent (sfa) would form around tiny drops of oil. The sfa was known to chemists as oleophobic, which meant that it repelled oil. After agitation, the result in tests had been an emulsfied oil mixture which had dispersed.

The tests, however, had involved some elements that weren't available where the *Torrey Canyon* went aground or where the oil from her holds went ashore. First of all, the detergent-emulsifying technique required that the detergent be applied in a very fine spray. After it had been sprayed on the slick, the slick had been agitated. In the test a small motorboat had run back and forth on the slick causing agitation from its propellers and from its wake.

The emulsified oil had then been thin enough for nature to take over. More than one hundred species of marine bacteria eat petroleum or, at least, that part of it made up of hydrocarbons. The problem here was the amount of oil the *Torrey Canyon* spilled. Under the best of circumstances, it would have taken months for bacteria to destroy that much oil. When the water temperature is below fifty degrees Fahrenheit, the bacteria stop eating oil, and the water temperature that chilly March wasn't much over fifty degrees.

But all military and naval people are taught that any action is better than none, so the spraying fleet was sent into action. Forty-two ships of various sizes were ordered to British navy docks for the installation of spraying equipment. When all the available ships had been equipped with the sprayers, fishing boats were chartered, equipped, and sent to the Seven Stones.

There were problems. Much of the equipment had been in dead storage for years. Some of it didn't work well, some of it didn't work at all, and some of the equipment was in the hands of people who had never seen a spraying machine before.

There had been an emergency call for the detergent itself. Very little of the specific kind of detergent for which the machines were intended was available. In the absence of anything

A U.S. Air Force airfield fire truck rushes to help clean up the Cornish coast. Here 55-gallon barrels of detergent are opened on top of the Cornish cliffs. U.S. AIR FORCE PHOTO.

better, a call for any kind of liquid detergent went out, and the call was met by twelve different kinds of detergent.

One thousand gallons of detergent—all the emergency stocks —went to the site of the wreck on the day it happened. The next day, 3,500 gallons of all kinds of detergent were used. British industry rose to the call and within 10 days of the wreck was delivering 100,000 gallons of detergent a day. About half of that was used on the Stones, and the other 50,000 gallons were used on the shoreline, the beaches, and the rocks.

Within three weeks 700,000 gallons of detergent had been used at sea. Perhaps less than half of this ocean of detergent had been sprayed as the plans called for. At least 40 percent and probably more was taken out to the slick and poured over the side. Most of this went right through the slick and settled on the bottom of the ocean. In the same three weeks 1,200,000 gallons had been used on the shore, and finding spraying equipment and getting it into place on the shore was even more difficult. About three-quarters of the shore-use detergent (900,000 gallons) was simply poured or dumped onto the beaches, the rocks, or into the shallow water.

The authorities and everyone else were acting in desperation. Not only was this the worst spill of all time, but the tides spreading the slick were the highest in 50 years. In some places oil was being splashed by huge waves as high as 30 feet up on the cliffs. The shores and beaches for a 140-mile stretch of the Cornish coast were polluted.

There was no pattern to the pollution. Some stretches of beach were completely free of any oil whatever, and other beaches a short distance away had crude oil many inches thick covering everything.

There was disagreement about what actually had happened and why. The British government named a committee of highly respected scientists to make an official report. Part of that committee's report said:

The main pollution of the Cornish Coast Line was caused by the 50,000 or so tons of crude oil which was released from the *Torrey Canyon* prior to her breakup. Assuming that a third of this was dispersed by evaporation and other natural processes, it is clear that the spraying with detergent prevented a considerable part of the remaining oil . . . from washing ashore. . . . It is estimated that only about 20,000 tons of oil finally reached the coast.

By implication, 700,000 gallons of detergent had successfully disposed of about 15,000 tons of oil at sea. (Twenty thousand tons reached the shoreline, and 15,000 tons [one-third of the

50,000 tons] dispersed naturally or through evaporation.) That claim ignored the manner in which the detergent was used (vast quantities were simply poured into the water, where it couldn't have done much good).

The British Marine Biological Association, a highly respected organization with no government connection, said in its report that about 21,000 tons of oil remained (from the first 50,000 tons dumped into the sea) after evaporation and that all of this wound up on the beaches of the Channel Islands and on the Brittany coast of France. Since 20,000 tons did land on the English coast, the Marine Biological Association cast doubt on the efficiency of both the detergent and the Royal Air Force and Royal Navy bombing of the *Torrey Canyon*.

The committee report said that it had "been proved" that bombing a ship like the *Torrey Canyon* to set the oil cargo on fire worked. Others said that few significant fires (there were spectacular fires set by the planes, but they became less spectacular when weighed against the amount of oil to be burned) were set and that there were no fires of "lasting duration."

In any event a week after the *Torrey Canyon* went aground, oil began to reach the Cornish beaches. On hand to meet it were hundreds of volunteers—adults, young people, and children, 75 Americans sent with pumping equipment by the United States Air Force from their normal duties as airfield firefighters, and 1,400 Royal Army soldiers and Royal Marines.

What came ashore was not what anyone expected, even oil men with previous spill experience. They had expected oil— dark, greenish-blue crude with the consistency of molasses. What they found was quickly nicknamed "chocolate mousse," because it was chocolate brown, light, stiff, and felt like mayonnaise. When the scientists examined it in laboratories, they found that it was a water-oil emulsion containing about 80 percent water. For lack of a better name, the emulsion was officially called chocolate mousse.

*Fire hoses now carrying detergent snake from a U.S. Air Force
pumper down to the Cornish beaches.* U.S. AIR FORCE PHOTO.

The first solution which occurred to practically everybody was to burn the oil. This didn't work. L. R. Benton, an expert employed by the British Petroleum Company, Ltd., reported that only oil in "neat pools" could be burned. When oil floating on the surface of the water was lighted, it burned just long enough to turn the water under it to steam; when the steam put the fire out. It was possible (but obviously impractical) to burn oil and chocolate mousse by the use of a military flamethrower. As long as the flamethrower was turned on, it would burn oil and chocolate mousse with its fuel; the minute the flamethrower was turned off, the fire went out.

Next somebody suggested that what was needed was wood shavings. These mixed with the oil would keep the mixture burning. This didn't work, either. Others went so far as to spread magnesium powder (which burns at exceedingly high temperatures) on the surface of the oil and then ignite the magnesium with a flare. As soon as the flare and magnesium powder were burned away, the fire went out.

The detergent, meanwhile, ordered on an emergency basis, began to arrive in enormous quantities, most of it packed in forty-five-gallon metal drums. Some of it was poured out of the drums into the surf. There were not enough sprayers around to be of much use, and so thousands of gallons were pumped, dribbled, and poured onto the beaches from hoses, hand pumps, and even garden watering cans. Helicopters made hundreds of flights loaded with forty-five-gallon drums, which they dropped out the door to burst on rocks.

What followed in many cases was greater pollution from the detergent. On one section of beach at Porthmere, for example, eager volunteers poured fifteen to twenty gallons of detergent onto every front foot of the beach. The stink that everybody complained about, according to Mr. Benton of British Petroleum, came from the detergent, not the oil.

And then the chocolate mousse arrived on the French coast,

where the French called it *la maree noire* (the black tide). The French accused the British of creating the mousse by the use of their detergent. They refused at first to use detergent at all and cleaned up their beaches with hard labor alone, physically removing the muck. They shoveled the chocolate mousse into pails and buckets and then dumped the buckets into ditches dug just beyond the beaches. Eventually the mousse separated; the water sank to the bottom of the ditch, and the oil on top was pumped out and burned.

When they could, the French also used a pumping vessel, the

A U. S. Air Force firefighter plays a stream of detergent on the rocks of the Cornish coast. U.S. AIR FORCE PHOTO.

motor ship *Petrobourg*. They would sail up to a patch of oil, put the side of the ship against it, and let the wind blow the oil against the side of the ship, where it built up to thicknesses of 60 centimeters (about 2 feet). Then the oil in the pileup was pumped aboard. This worked only as long as the sea was very calm. The minute the waves reached a foot or so in height and the ship bobbed up and down, the pump would either suck water from below the oil slick or air from above it and take oil aboard only in that short period when the mouth of the suction hose was actually in the oil. Nevertheless, the French managed to pick up (and keep away from the beaches) some 6,000 tons of oil with the *Petrobourg*.

In England, meanwhile, a product of American technology arrived in a specially chartered jet from the United States. Costing $67,000, it was a plastic boom, which, when stretched across the surface of the sea, would gather oil, permit it to be pumped up, and keep it from passing and reaching the beaches. It lasted about an hour in the water before the seagulls found out that it was edible and ate it.

French student volunteers at the French Maritime Biological Station at Roscoff did far better with their homemade booms. They filled burlap bags with straw and wood shavings and tied them together. They held back the oil, but their success was based at least in part on unusually smooth seas. Any sort of a wave action would have splashed over the fragile booms and torn them apart.

The most successful French technique was the use of straw and strawlike materials rolled up and laid the length of a beach. As the tide came in with the oil floating on top of it, it splashed over the straw. The water ran out, and the oil was caught in the straw. The tide pushed the straw farther up the beach as it came in. Then the oil straw was collected and burned or sometimes just burned on the spot.

The French had great success off Biscay Bay, where they sank

20,000 tons of oil in 1,000 feet of water by using stearated chalk grandly called *craie de Champagne.* They dumped 3,000 tons of the chalk onto an oil slick containing 23,500 tons of oil and sank most of it, for a fraction of the $560,000 it had cost the British to spray and dump detergents in the area of the *Torrey Canyon* alone. (Far more detergent was used on the Cornish coast.)

The British had been flatly against using any sinking technique to get rid of the oil, because they believed that sunken oil would seriously, and for a very long time, pollute the bottom of the sea, destroying marine life of all sorts. The British are not any more eager to admit they've made a mistake than anyone else, but J. Wardley Smith, senior principal scientific officer of the Watten Spring (marine biological) Laboratory came close to admitting he was wrong when he told a symposium of the British Institute of Petroleum, "It has been found that the natural biological degradation of oil in the sea . . . is much more rapid than at first believed," and, "it is necessary to reconsider the general problem of sinking oil using powdered solids."

The birds suffered most from the *Torrey Canyon* disaster, which came at the worst possible time for the razorbills, great northern divers, guillemots, shags, puffins, and other seabirds which breed on the southern coast of England. They were in the midst of their spring migration. Oil destroys the natural insulation of bird feathers, and oil-soaked birds by the thousands (estimates range from ten thousand to twenty-five thousand) died either of exposure or of starvation because they were too exhausted by exposure to hunt for food.

People tried to help them. More than 7,000 oil-soaked birds were captured and lovingly bathed and set free again. Realistic biologists said that fewer than 1 percent, or 70, birds ever returned to their normal life patterns.

When the crude was dumped into the sea, it was poisonous. But the toxic parts of the crude were those parts which evaporated first; what was left after a couple of days was a crude oil of little potential danger to marine life. Within four months the danger to anything was completely gone as the oil was devoured by marine bacteria.

Dr. W. Gunkel of the (German) biological institute at Helogland rushed to England and France to see what he could learn about the effects of the spill to stockpile knowledge against a future spill in German waters. Using a self-designed counting device he found 400 million oil-decomposing bacteria in 1 cubic centimeter of oil-soaked Cornwall sand. In calm, scientific language he allowed that this was indeed "high bacterial activity." The oil, in other words, would revert to nature far more quickly than anyone had supposed if it were not interfered with.

Gunkel and others also found that the detergent had not only proven more lethal to marine life than the oil it was intended to disperse, but that the toxic portion of the detergent had been the kerosene-based solvent. Fortunately, this had evaporated first and quickly. The Plymouth scientists committee said that if the solvent had not quickly evaporated, "the biological consequences to the English channel would have been vastly worse than they were."

There was no decrease in seafood because of the spill. The lobster catch in 1967 remained about what it had been in 1966 (1,600) and crabs caught went up from 15,700 to 20,500. In deeper waters the mackerel catch went up from 30,000 hundredweight in 1966 to 43,800 in 1967 after the *Torrey Canyon* spill.

When the mess was finally cleaned up, after thousands of hours of miserable hard labor at a painfully high cost, the scientists sat down to draw conclusions based on what they had learned. They concluded, among other things, that detergents were not the only answer and, indeed, were often the wrong answer. If it were possible (and obviously it would often not be possible), the best thing to do would be to follow the French lead of sinking oil slicks before they reached the shoreline. The oil which did reach the shoreline should be left there for nature to handle, if possible. If this isn't possible (when the beach is needed for the use of people in the summer, for example) then a careful application of no more detergent than is needed, using the proper equipment, operated by trained personnel, may be necessary.

In other words, there should be no more wholesale dumping of a miracle cure into the water by well-meaning but untrained people. If possible, the report concluded, the oil reaching the shore should be left in place, and nature should be helped to cleanse itself by merely plowing the beach from time to time to insure that the bacteria eating the oil get enough oxygen.

A year after the *Torrey Canyon* disaster, America had its first major oil spill. The *Ocean Eagle* went aground off San Juan harbor in Puerto Rico. The United States Coast Guard under the law (the Coast Pollution Act of 1961) immediately began to spray the oil slicks with various chemicals.

Four days later, however, acting on the advice of the United States Water Pollution Control Administration, the governor of Puerto Rico, under his executive authority, issued a cease-and-desist order to the coast guard. The detergent the coast guard had been using had turned the heavy Venezuelan crude oil into large lumps heavier than the sea water, and they had sunk, endangering marine life. What followed was a technique based partly on what we had learned from the English and French after *Torrey Canyon* and partly on American ingenuity.

We floated chicken-wire baskets filled with absorbent material both to stop the oil from reaching the beaches and to collect as much of it as possible. The weather was with us, and we were able to pump 45,000 gallons of oil a day from the smooth surface of San Juan Bay for disposal. We built wire-mesh sleds and skidded them across the seabed to pick up the large lumps of crude the coast guard had sunk. We devised a new type of absorbent—crushed and treated volcanic rock—and spread this on the surface of the oil slicks. When that washed ashore, it was a fairly easy (if still dirty and miserable) job to collect it for disposal.

It wasn't a complete success. More than nine thousand cubic meters of San Juan's famous beach sand had to be hauled away because it was oil soaked. Everybody was inconvenienced. But there was no massive kill of marine life or seabirds, and six months after the spill the coast guard reported that things were back to normal except for oil-stained rocks. The tides at the time of the *Ocean Eagle* grounding, as they had been for the *Torrey Canyon*, had gone into the record books.

None of this is intended to suggest that oil spills, either from huge tankers or from pipelines, are insignificant. They are, in fact, one of the more frightening aspects of our life today, and it is unpleasant to consider that we haven't seen the last of them.

But the alternative of doing without oil, that dirty brown substance which has enriched the lives of each one of us beyond anything the founding fathers of this country could conceive, is unthinkable. What the disasters and pollution may be telling us, however, is that people must always pay for what they get, even if they get it "free" from the earth.

chapter 17

IN 1973 THE UNITED STATES AND THE WORLD SUD-
denly became aware of an "energy crisis," although the president
of the United States refused to use that term because he felt the
problem hadn't reached the point where it could properly be
called a crisis. What the energy problem did, if nothing else,
was to help get people to think in terms of energy, rather than in
terms of coal or electricity or oil. There is an "oil shortage" only
because people use so much oil in their inefficient conversion of
oil into energy. If people used oil solely for its lubricating
qualities, there would be no problem at all.

What, then, is energy? And where are we going to get energy
if we are going to exhaust our oil this century or the next century? Or if, a century or two after that, we exhaust our coal?
Albert Einstein, a one-time class dunce now universally regarded as one of the greatest mathematicians of all time, came
up with a simple formula for energy: $E=MC^2$.

The simplicity of the formula is deceptive, and the practical
application of the formula is something that people have just
begun to work at. What Einstein said was that matter and
energy are simply different manifestations of the same force and
thus are interchangeable.

Einstein's theory holds that if one gram of matter were converted to its other form, energy (E in the equation), the resulting force would be equal to the amount of matter (M in the equation) multiplied by the square of the speed of energy (C^2). The speed of energy is the speed of light—186,000 miles per second.

An erg is a unit of force measurement. To move 1 gram 1 centimeter in 1 second requires 1 erg of force. A centimeter (1/100 of a meter) is about .39 inch. A gram is about .033 ounce. An erg, obviously, isn't much force.

Converting the speed of energy to the metric system of measurement gives us a speed of 300,000 kilometers per second. A kilometer is 1,000 meters, and a centimeter is 1/1000 of a meter. Thus the speed of energy/light is 300,000,000,000 centimeters per second. The square of that figure is 90,000,000,-000,000,000,000.

A little more simple arithmetic will show that, according to Einstein, there is enough energy in one gram of matter to move 7 million tons 1 mile in 1 second. People (by nuclear fission) have managed to convert some matter into energy, but the efficiency with which they have done it so far is quite crude compared to the efficiency with which the sun converts matter into energy.

The sun, the scientists tell us, converts 425 million tons of matter into energy every minute. Phrased another way, the sun radiates 60,000–75,000 horsepower per square yard of surface continually. It radiates in all directions, of course, and only a small, barely definable portion of the total energy has reached earth, but that has been enough to provide every square mile of earth with about 5 million horsepower, and the sun, of course, is still radiating energy.

All energy on earth comes from the sun. People have always been faced with the problem of converting that energy to their use but so far have done so only in very inefficient ways, most conspicuously by burning the fossil fuels, coal and petroleum, for their heat, which is not the same thing as their total energy. They have learned only in the last twenty years, for example, to generate electricity in minute amounts by applying the sun's rays to a silicon device we call a "solar cell." The atom wasn't split until 1943, and ten years before that, people weren't even sure what the atom was.

Ninety percent of the scientists and engineers who ever lived are alive today. What's going to happen scientifically in the next week or the next twenty years or the next century is obviously going to make the citizens of the next century look back with smug superiority on the citizens of this century, exactly as we feel a little smug about our great-grandparents, who had neither electricity, penicillin, nor the automobile, not to mention television and the atom bomb.

But what about the immediate future? What about satisfying our requirements, which grow daily, for energy in our lifetime?

The other fossil fuel, coal, offers the most likely solution to the problem for the immediate future. The known reserves of coal are so enormous that even the most dedicated pessimist has to admit we're not liable to run out of it in the next three or four hundred years.

One of the reasons for the "oil shortage" now is that environmentalists (quite properly) have drawn public attention to the air pollution caused by the combustion of coal at the power plants, which put impurities (notably sulphur) into the air. So oil, which burns "cleanly," was diverted to the power plants to replace coal.

Getting the sulphur (and other impurities) out of coal is a problem. But to a society which has come in three-quarters of a century from the Wright brothers to astronauts on the moon, finding an efficient, economical way to extract one chemical substance from a fossil fuel before it is burned (or while burning it) does not seem to be an insoluble problem.

Science has already learned how to make oil (and thus gasoline) from coal. The process is expensive and at the moment, prohibitively so. But that doesn't mean that a cheaper process cannot or will not be developed.

Nuclear fission—or the heat generated by the process—is another possible solution. Cost is one problem, and disposal of radioactive wastes is another. The important point is that nuclear generating plants are, right now, providing a source of energy and that expansion of their capability is a matter of technique and improvement, not something requiring a whole new science.

Another source of energy waiting to be tapped is the heat of the earth itself. Just a few short miles under the earth's surface are sources of heat providing extremely high temperatures (1,000 degrees Fahrenheit and up) which scientists are today trying to tap. Getting at those sources isn't as simple as running a steam pipe into the ground, of course, and the scientists are facing awesome difficulties. They haven't been at the problem very long, however, and there is no reason to believe that they'll fail to find a workable technology.

But, for the immediate future, it seems certain that people are going to be able to get all the energy they need from petroleum. They may well have to drill oil wells where they have never been drilled before, probably on the floor of the sea and to greater depths beneath the surface of the earth, but people will drill them and find oil. And, for the foreseeable future, humanity will continue to take its energy from the fascinating petrocarbon compound we call oil.

Index